AMEBOID MOVEMENT

LECTOR HOUSE PUBLIC DOMAIN WORKS

HAPPY READING!

AMEBOID MOVEMENT

ASA ARTHUR SCHAEFFER

ISBN: 978-93-89560-08-4

Published: 1920

LECTOR HOUSE LLP
E-MAIL: lectorpublishing@gmail.com

AMEBOID MOVEMENT

BY

ASA A. SCHAEFFER, Ph.D.

PROFESSOR OF ZOOLOGY, UNIVERSITY
OF TENNESSEE

1920

PREFACE

Although the subject of ameboid movement is discussed in this book chiefly because of its intrinsic interest, yet the interests of the student of medicine, the psychologist, the physiologist, the evolutionist and the general biologist have constantly been kept in mind. For the medical investigator probably finds no better means of approach to the study of the reactions and especially the movements of the white blood corpuscles, which play such an important part in the economy of the human body, than the ameba; white blood corpuscles and amebas are strikingly similar in many characteristics and in the fundamental processes of the movement they are probably identical. The comparative psychologist is keenly interested in the activities of the ameba because it exhibits to him the operation of the animal mind in its greatest simplicity. To the physiologist ameboid movement has for a long time represented the simplest phase of muscular contraction as it is known in the vertebrates. The philosophical evolutionist sees in the ameba, both in its structure and in its activities, a close approximation to the earliest ancestor of the animals. And the general biologist, aside from his usual interest in the properties of living matter wherever it may be found, is especially interested in discovering how many of the activities of the ameba are common to other organisms.

But in addition to presenting an account of the main facts concerned in the movement of the ameba from the various points of view mentioned above, this book has a second object which is scarcely subsidiary to the main one. This second object is to present the thesis that moving organisms in which orienting organs are absent or not functioning, always move in orderly paths, i. e., in helical or true spiral paths. The movements of the ameba under controlled conditions, which, as the following pages will show, take the form of a helical spiral projected on a plane surface, therefore serve as an introductory study to the movements of organisms generally. For the presumption is strong that there is an innate tendency in all organisms that move which compels them, when free from stimulation, to move in definite predictable paths. This thesis is discussed at some length in Chapters XII and XIII.

In view of the fact that ameboid movement has been considered largely as a theoretical question heretofore, I wish to state at once that my discussion of this subject is based directly on observation and experiment. I have no new theory of ameboid movement to offer; the list of theories is already extensive enough. I am, on the other hand, strongly of the opinion that this fundamental question, if it is to be solved at all, can be solved only by persistent observation and experiment on the ameba and related organisms themselves. "All knowledge is vain and erroneous excepting that brought into the world by sense perception, the mother of all certainty" (Leonardo).

CONTENTS

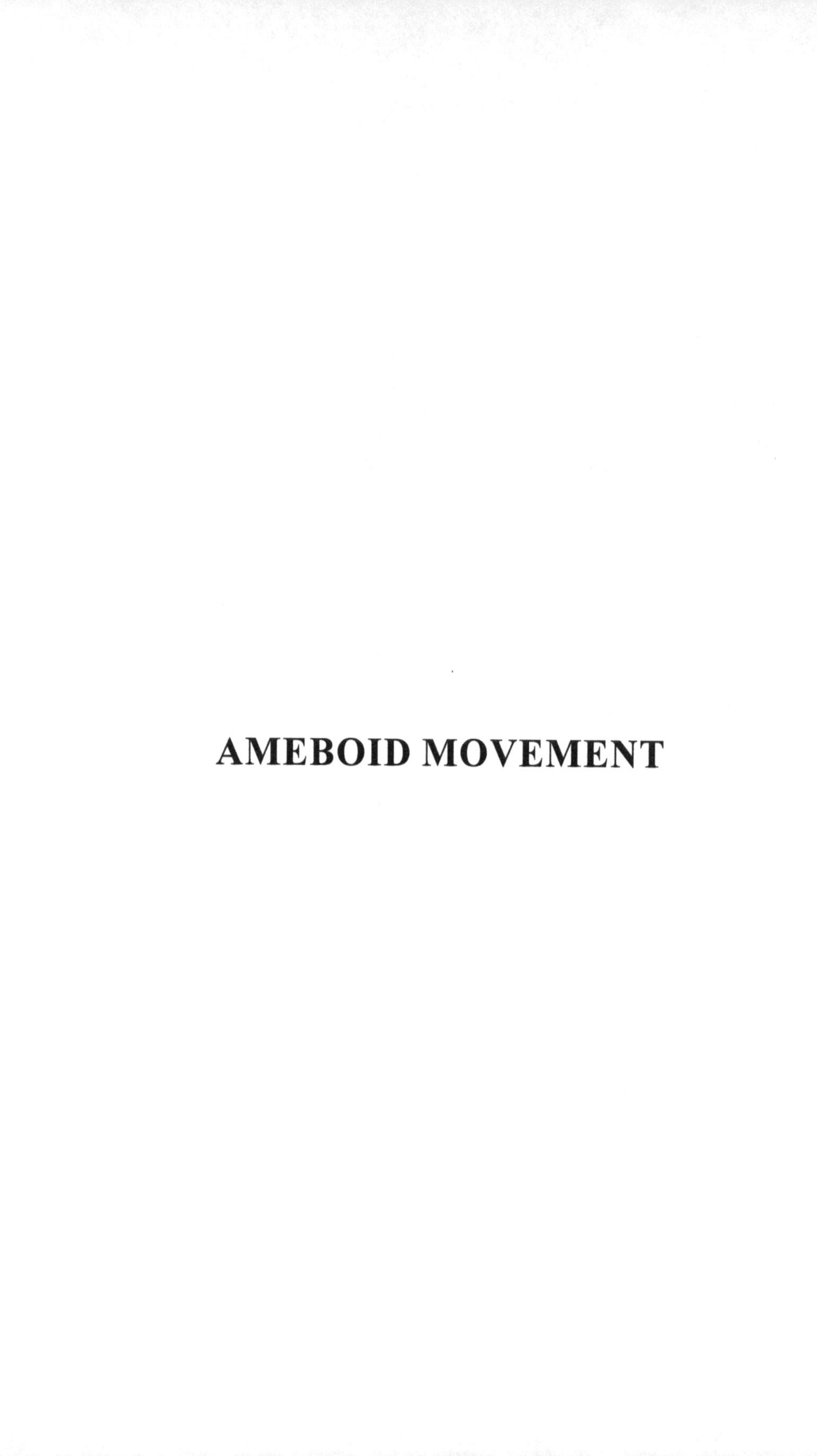

AMEBOID MOVEMENT

CHAPTER I

INTRODUCTION

The manner of movement common to amebas has attracted the attention of biologists ever since the discovery of ameba by Rösel v. Rosenhof in 1755. In his description of "Der kleine Proteus" he records the observation that the various form changes which the ameba undergoes are associated with the streaming of the endoplasm. This observation marks the very beginning of the investigation of ameboid movement. And this investigation also possesses the distinction of being the most important single observation that has thus far been recorded in this special field, for it is now generally understood that by ameboid movement is meant movement due to the streaming of protoplasm.

The phenomenon of ameboid movement as discovered by v. Rosenhof, was an isolated phenomenon. It attracted attention mainly because of its uniqueness, for it was the only instance of the kind that was then known. It could not be compared with any other form of movement; and the animal itself, considered apart from the streaming of the protoplasm, was unique also, because of its remarkable form changes which it alone, of all the animals then known, exhibited.

But when Corti in 1774 discovered streaming protoplasm in the cells of chara and various other plants, the ameba could no longer be said to occupy this position of isolation. Although streaming is not accompanied by locomotion in chara, it had been observed that movement in the ameba was always accompanied by streaming, so it came to be generally accepted that the really fundamental feature of ameboid movement was the streaming of the protoplasm.

The ameba came to be of especial interest to the physiologists later on when the finer structures of the larger animals were studied more carefully. Thus when the normal movements of the white blood corpuscles were discovered, no one failed to be struck with their ameboid characteristics in almost every detail of movement, feeding habits and gross structure. The great importance of the functions that have been ascribed to leukocytes, and their very widespread occurrence in the higher animals has served to give rise to the belief that ameboid characteristics were not unique among animals, but common to many of them. The discovery of ameboid movements among plant zoospores, among animal ova, in the endoderm cells lining the digestive tract of a great variety of animals, in the nuclei of some animal cells, in the wandering cells of sponges and other animals—all these instances of ameboid movement occurring in such widely different tissues inevitably placed it among the most important phenomena known to occur in organisms.

Out of the discovery that ameboid movement may be exhibited in some form or other in so many different kinds of organisms, grew the theory that even muscular movement as known in man and the higher animals is at bottom a specialized sort of ameboid movement; not merely phylogenetically, but as it is now known. As we shall see however in the following pages, this theory of muscular movement cannot be based specifically on the streaming process per se, but it is very probable, on the other hand, that the same process which underlies contraction of the ectoplasm in the ameba also underlies contraction in muscular tissue.

But this remarkable story of the development of a single unrelated observation into a widespread biological phenomenon is not yet complete. With its further development the following pages are concerned. It will be shown that the movement of the surface film of the ameba is analogous to that of some blue-green algae, diatoms and crawling euglenas, in which organisms the surface film seems to be the vehicle of movement. Thus the ameba finds itself related to these organisms by new ties. More important still is the significance of the wavy path of the ameba, which may possibly be due to the same fundamental mechanism that controls, under suitable conditions, the direction of the path in man and many other animals and motile plant cells. Thus the phenomenon of ameboid movement born in nakedness and utter isolation, has become attired, in a brief space, with the Victorian garb of a Fundamental.

CHAPTER II
HISTORICAL SKETCH

For the purpose of presenting in brief compass the main published observations and experiments on ameboid movement, we may pass from the observations of v. Rosenhof, mentioned in the introduction, to certain observations which Wallich ('63) recorded. He found that a new pseudopod is usually formed as a small break in the ectoplasm somewhere on the ameba through which the endoplasm then flows. As the endoplasm flows out and the new pseudopod enlarges, the breach in the ectoplasm increases in extent, through a transformation of the ectoplasm in the immediate vicinity of the breach, into endoplasm. But he observed also that some of the endoplasm which flows into the new pseudopod becomes transformed into ectoplasm. Wallich thus demonstrated that ectoplasm and endoplasm are mutually convertible.

The conversion of ectoplasm into endoplasm and vice versa, was regarded by Wallich, however, as a process taking place only occasionally, such as when new pseudopods are formed. It remained for Bütschli ('80, p. 115) to point out that in a moving ameba endoplasm is continually formed from ectoplasm at the anterior ends of all pseudopods, while the reverse process, viz., the conversion of ectoplasm into endoplasm, takes place continually at the posterior end of the ameba. He describes the relation of ectoplasm to endoplasm as a "circulation"; the endoplasm, arriving at the anterior end, becomes changed into ectoplasm, which after remaining relatively stationary for a while on the outer side of the animal, soon finds itself at the posterior end of the ameba, where it is slowly changed into endoplasm. The movement of the endoplasm forward to the anterior end of the ameba completes the cycle.

In 1898 Rhumbler, from observations on several species of amebas, came to the conclusion that in the *change* from ectoplasm into endoplasm, and vice versa, must be sought the cause of ameboid movement.

Jennings ('04), however, from extended study of the physiology of the ameba, stressing especially movement and feeding, denied that the transformation of endoplasm into ectoplasm, and vice versa, is necessary or even of frequent occurrence during movement. Instead of these transformations occurring regularly, as Bütschli and Rhumbler described them, Jennings concluded that the ectoplasm is more or less permanent, behaving like an elastic skin, which rolls over and over as the ameba moves along. The ectoplasm thus remains ectoplasm, and the endoplasm retains its identity, for considerable periods of time, instead of being continually transformed, the one into the other, as the ameba moves along.

Although observations with regard to movement in ameba have consisted almost wholly of the mutual relations of ectoplasm and endoplasm, it is important to note that the existence of a *third layer* of protoplasm, outside of the ectoplasm, was foreshadowed by an observation of Bütschli ('92, p. 219) while examining a pelomyxa. To his great surprise he found that there were currents of water, as evidenced by the movement of suspended particles, at the sides and in close contact with the ectoplasm of the pelomyxa, which flowed slowly forwards toward the anterior end. No details were given and no explanation offered for the cause of the currents excepting the suggestion that there might be a thin skin over the animal, which moves slowly forward.

Two years later Blochmann ('94) demonstrated by means of the very fine cilia-like projections which frequently cover the outside of pelomyxas, that the surface of the pelomyxa actually moves forward during active locomotion. He did not state definitely whether or not he considered this surface as a part of the ectoplasm.

This observation of Blochmann was not developed, however, until Jennings ('04), by means of particles attached to the outer surface of amebas, studied the forward movement of this layer. The results of Jennings' work led him to conclude that the outer surface of amebas, which move forward as demonstrated by attached particles of soot and other substances, is continuous with the ectoplasm, and is really the ectoplasm. The rate of movement of this layer was stated to be about the same as that of the ameba as a whole. He denied the validity of Bütschli's suggestion that there might be a thin third layer on the outside of amebas or pelomyxas.

But the existence of a third layer of protoplasm as distinct from the ectoplasm, was again maintained by Schaeffer ('17) who found that in some amebas the outer surface moves forward faster than the ameba advances through the water. The third layer was found to be generated over the surface of the ameba, especially in the posterior region of the ameba, and destroyed at the anterior end.

But the purely observational aspect of the problem of ameboid movement has not interested biologists generally as much as the ultimate cause of the phenomenon.

The first attempt that was made to explain ameboid movement in conformity with the demands of modern experimental science, that is, on the basis of physical factors, was made by Berthold ('86). By means of simple experiments with inert fluids (oils, alcohol, water, ether) which were modeled after an experiment described by the physicist Paalzow ('58), Berthold concluded that locomotion in ameboid organisms is due to the physical attraction of the anterior end to the substratum. The ameba was supposed to behave like a drop of fluid which moved towards the point where the tension of the ameba's surface was decreased by contact with the substratum. The ameba did not *push out* pseudopods according to Berthold, but they were *pulled out* because of a difference in surface tension between them and the substratum. But pseudopods which were extended into the water and out of contact with a solid substratum, were said to be extended by a contractile effort of the posterior region of the ameba.

Bütschli ('92, p. 187) pointed out that it was highly improbable that pseudopods in contact with a solid substratum were projected in a fundamentally different way from that in which free pseudopods were extended, as explained by Berthold. Bütschli assumed that all ameboid movement was due to the same fundamental cause. He postulated surface tension as the active agent, as Berthold had done for the extension of pseudopods in contact with a solid substrate; but Bütschli assumed that the decrease in surface tension at the anterior end of the ameba was brought about by the bursting of protoplasmic droplets of a more fluid consistency on the surface of the ameba, the consistency of which was less fluid, thus bringing about a decrease of surface tension and consequent forward streaming of the endoplasm. The necessary migration of the more fluid droplets to the surface was determined by internal conditions. The direction in which an ameba moves was assumed to depend therefore not upon the physical character of the substrate, as suggested by Berthold, but upon such internal changes as control the movement of the more liquid part of the internal protoplasm to the outer surface.

Rhumbler ('98) wrote extensively on the subject of ameboid movement, especially from the point of view of the feeding habits of amebas. He concluded that the flow of protoplasm, while engulfing a food object, was a direct result of the lowering of the surface tension of the protoplasm by contact with the food object (p. 207), thus causing its envelopment. Numerous other writers of the time, including Quincke ('88), Verworn ('89, '92), Blochmann ('94), Bernstein ('00) and Jensen ('02), agreed in a general way with Rhumbler's position that surface tension changes are the cause of locomotion in ameba.

In 1904 the general subject of ameban behavior was extensively studied by Jennings, and from his observations he concluded that surface tension cannot account for many of the reactions observed. Other factors, he held, must be at work, such as contractility, which, acting in the posterior region, causes the endoplasm to flow forward. But Jennings found it impossible to explain on the same basis the extension of free pseudopods, and the creeping of a pseudopod, or of the whole ameba, over a solid substratum.

From further observations Rhumbler ('05, '10) came to modify his earlier views as stated above. The rapid advances in the study of the chemistry of colloids doubtless suggested to Rhumbler that the change from endoplasm to ectoplasm resembled the change from a sol to a gel state, and that in this process of gelation lay the source of energy manifested in ameboid movement. In thus calling attention to, and emphasizing the colloidal nature of, the conversion of endoplasm into ectoplasm and vice versa, the problem of ameboid movement came to be discussed from an entirely new angle. Certain phases of Rhumbler's theory are developed and elaborated by Hyman ('17) who agrees in general with Rhumbler's conclusions.

In a series of papers on feeding and other reactions of ameba, Schaeffer ('12, '16, '17) concluded that Rhumbler's general statement, wherein he says that changes in behavior are directly deducible from the action of stimuli in effecting liquefaction or gelation of the ectoplasm, does not hold in many cases of feeding, and that the mechanism controlling locomotion and feeding is not external, as maintained by Rhumbler, but internal.

CHAPTER III

THE GENERAL FEATURES OF ENDOPLASMIC STREAMING

The streaming of the endoplasm is the most conspicuous feature of ameboid movement. It is even more noticeable than the movement of the pseudopods themselves, because of its greater speed and because it occurs in all parts of the ameba. Its importance in movement is essential, for no continued locomotion can be observed unless accompanied by streaming. It may be profitable therefore to enquire into the general features of streaming, and to observe some of the necessary consequences streaming imposes upon such an animal as the ameba.

Let us take as an example an *Amoeba proteus* (Pallas, '66, emend. Leidy, '79, emend. Schaeffer, '16) in characteristic movement (see Figure 11, p. 37). The main streams of endoplasm are in the same direction as that in which the ameba moves. In the withdrawing pseudopods the current is, of course, toward the main mass of the ameba. The endoplasmic stream is continuous from the posterior end to the tips of the advancing pseudopods. The retracting pseudopods flow into the main stream as tributaries. If, as often happens, the ameba is without pseudopods, there is then a single stream arising in the posterior end and flowing to the anterior end. In such a case it is readily observed how absolutely dependent locomotion is upon endoplasmic streaming.

It often happens, such as when the ameba is receiving a strong stimulus, that streaming is arrested and brought to a stop for a few seconds, more or less. Presently however the endoplasm begins to flow as before. At what point, in such a case, is the first movement of endoplasm detectible? Is it at the free end of the pseudopod, at its middle region, at its base, or at the posterior end of the ameba? Bütschli ('80, p. 116) observed that in a withdrawing pseudopod the streaming begins at the free end of the pseudopod; but his ('92, p. 201) later explanation of ameboid movement seems to require that the endoplasm must begin to move at the base of the withdrawing pseudopod. Jennings ('04, p. 157) observed that in a withdrawing pseudopod the current of endoplasm begins at the base of the pseudopod.

From numerous observations directed toward this point, it appears that the conditions under which streaming is resumed after a pause, whether in the same or in the reverse direction, are of great variety. The shape, size, slenderness, and the position on the ameba of the pseudopod, as well as the strength and character of the stimulus, are among the factors capable of changing in whole or in part the flow of endoplasm in a pseudopod. In an ameba that has been moving along a homogeneous flat surface, as nearly unstimulated as may be, the endoplasm first begins to flow out of the lower half of the retracting pseudopod, if the pseudopod is more or less uniformly conical in shape and rather slender. In such a case it may be said that the retracting pseudopod was withdrawn "by the ameba," and that it did not itself receive an external stimulus producing retraction. If, however, the tip of a pseudopod as described receives a strong negative stimulus, the endoplasm frequently flows back from the tip while it is still flowing into the pseudopod at the base. But very soon thereafter, in such an event, the streaming becomes unified and the pseudopod is withdrawn. In broad pseudopods about to be withdrawn, the endoplasm may begin to move anywhere along its length. This is undoubtedly due to the continuous local changes in the walls of the pseudopod, which are characteristic of this species of ameba (see p. 20).

In an ameba which has been brought to a standstill, as by a sudden flash of light, the first sign of recurring streaming is in the anterior half, whether the original direction of streaming is resumed or reversed. If the direction is reversed, the active pseudopods retract for a considerable distance before a new one is projected. The endoplasmic stream in a slender withdrawing pseudopod may not reach to the tip for from several seconds to a minute, if the tip is slightly positively stimulated. One may then observe ectoplasm streaming toward the tip and toward the base, in the respective regions, at the same time, with considerable fluctuation back and forth of the neutral zone separating the two streams. The fate of such a pseudopod depends on its size, on its position on the ameba, and the strength of the stimulus affecting it and the rest of the ameba. That is, if the pseudopod is small or on the posterior half of the ameba, or only slightly stimulated, it will be retracted; but if it is large, or on the anterior end of the ameba, or more strongly stimulated than the rest of the ameba, it may again become active.

The fact that protoplasm is practically incompressible makes it clear that if streaming can be observed to begin after a pause at some point after it begins at others, the ectoplasmic walls of the ameba must give way in the region where streaming begins. Since it has been established by observation that the ectoplasm may give way at any point, it follows that one of the principal factors affecting streaming is the elasticity and liquefiability of the ectoplasm.

The streaming in an ameba is coordinated. The direction in which the endoplasm flows in the several pseudopods, when there are no stimuli received externally that produce visible changes in behavior, gives one the impression that there is a "centre" controlling movement. The several pseudopods do not act at all capriciously. The ameba seems to move the pseudopods, not the pseudopods the ameba. If this impression of coordination is correct, it is of the first importance in a study of ameboid movement. Further on, this point will be taken up at length in connection with the character of the path an externally unstimulated ameba describes (p. 109); but there are certain observations which aid in the analysis of the problem of coördination from the point of view of the pseudopod, instead of that of the ameba as a whole, and to these observations we may now direct our attention.

The mass of endoplasm within a pseudopod moves practically always in one direction. In any cross-section of a pseudopod that is more or less cylindrical in shape, the endoplasm in the center moves most rapidly, that near to it less rapidly, while that near the ectoplasm moves very slowly. One never observes a forward stream on one side of the pseudopod and a backward stream on the other. Nor does one observe parallel streams of endoplasm flowing in opposite directions within the same ectoplasmic tube, in an ameba of several pseudopods, excepting where there is a wide zone of stationary endoplasm between the streams (Figure 1, *v, w*).

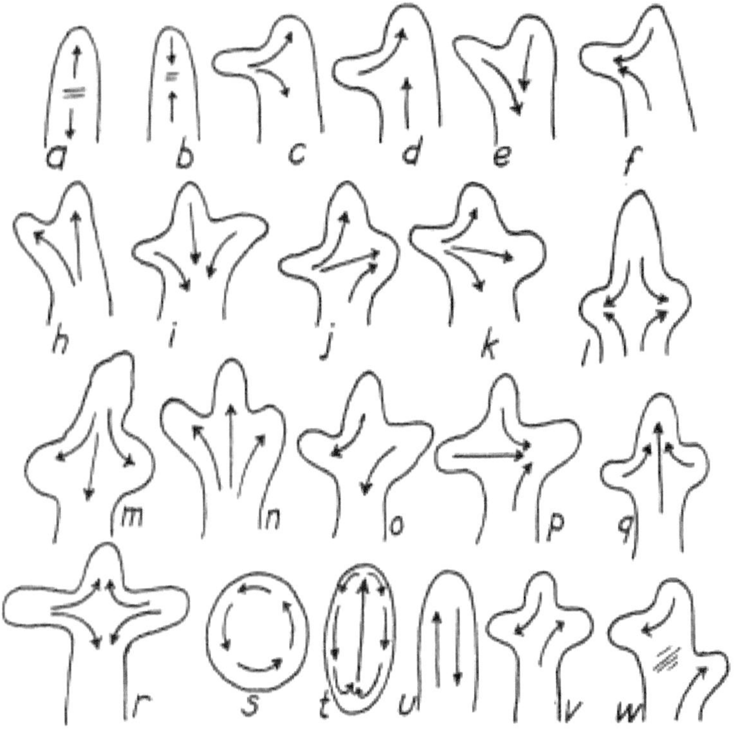

FIGURE 1.

Illustrating the various directions of endoplasmic streaming in growing and retracting pseudopods. a, two oppositely directed streams in a pseudopod, one directed toward the base and the other toward the tip of the pseudopod, with a neutral zone between. b, two streams flowing toward each other. Cases c to r are self explanatory. s, rotational currents observed occasionally in various species of amebas. t, "fountain currents," sometimes observed in Amoeba blattae, and rarely in other forms. u and v represent cases of streaming which have not been observed and which probably do not occur. w, similar to v, but with a wide neutral zone between the streams, represents an actual observed case. m and r probably occur only very rarely; no such cases have been seen, but there seems to be no reason why they do not sometimes occur. Excepting m, u, r and v, all these figures were drawn from observed cases of streaming.

But in "fountain currents," such as Rhumbler ('98, p. 190) described and figured for *Amoeba blattae* Bütschli, and which may readily be observed in most species of amebas if immersed in a solution of gelatin thick enough to keep the amebas from sinking, there is a central stream of endoplasm flowing forward, and a peripheral stream of ectoplasm flowing backward, with a thin neutral zone between (Figure 29, *d*). As we shall see further on, however, these fountain currents are in principle the same as the currents observed in ordinary locomotion, the apparent difference being due to the fact that there is no locomotion. It is true, then, that within the same pseudopod at any cross section the endoplasm always streams in one direction, and the streaming is unified.

When new pseudopods are formed, or when old ones are retracted, and especially when both these phenomena occur at the same time and close together on a part of an older pseudopod, some of the details of coordination in streaming are readily made out. In Figure 1 are shown a number of observed cases of pseudopod formation and retraction, with the direction of endoplasmic streams indicated at a given instant. For the purpose of illustration, several (presumably) possible but unobserved cases, *m* and *r*, are sketched, and also two cases, *u* and *v*, which have not been observed and which probably do not occur. The general conclusion to be drawn from these observations is that, while the endoplasm in the body of an ameba as a whole may be streaming in several different directions at any given instant, that is almost never the case with an individual pseudopod, especially if the pseudopod is of small or medium size and not too flat or otherwise irregular in shape. The pseudopod is therefore the unit of coordinated protoplasmic streaming.

Another general observation which undoubtedly is connected in some way with the problem of coordinated streaming is the following. In externally unstimulated amebas, the new pseudopods are almost without exception directed 60° or less from the direction in which the parent pseudopods are moving.

It is a matter of common observation that an ameba may throw out a pseudopod in any direction whatsoever when stimulated. The ameba may reverse its direction of movement completely, or it may move in scores of different directions at one time for awhile, if properly stimulated. There is no restraint or limit imposed upon the ameba insofar as the direction of movement is concerned. Why then should a great majority of new pseudopods in an unstimulated ameba be projected at an angle of approximately 60° to the parent pseudopod? It might seem at first sight as if the merely physical aspect of the streaming would be a sufficient explanation, in that less resistance would be met with in sending a stream off at a small angle than at a large. But it is probable that inertia plays no part in maintaining the direction of streaming (see p. 123, footnote, for further discussion). It requires perhaps more energy for a pseudopod to flow off from the main stream at an angle of 120° than at an angle of 30°. But it is plain that as many pseudopods are withdrawn as are thrown out, and they are withdrawn at an angle against the main stream of endoplasm in the ameba that is the complement of the angle at which they were projected. Whatever energy might be saved therefore in the projection of a new pseudopod at a small angle with the main stream is lost in withdrawing the pseudopod against the stream at a correspondingly large angle. It is clear therefore that the physics of moving viscous fluids cannot solve the problem. It is probable that the mechanism which controls the direction of locomotion as exemplified in the wavy path of the ameba (see p. 109) is also involved in the direction in which pseudopods are projected.

Some very interesting special cases of endoplasmic streaming are observed during the process of feeding. As is well known, amebas capture their food by the protoplasm flowing around it and engulfing it. If the object is large the protoplasm may flow around it, in contact with it, so that the shape of the object determines the direction in which the enveloping protoplasm flows. If the object is small, particularly if it is a live organism, the behavior of the ameba is quite different (Kepner and Taliaferro, '13, Schaeffer, '16). To capture such a food object a cup of protoplasm is gradually formed over it so as to imprison it (Figure 2). If the food organism lies against some flat object, the food cup is brought down to the surface of the object all around, thus making escape impossible, before the protoplasm comes into contact with the food organism. Schaeffer ('16, '18) by experimental methods has shown that the stimulus calling forth the formation of food cups as just described, is the mechanical vibration of the water.

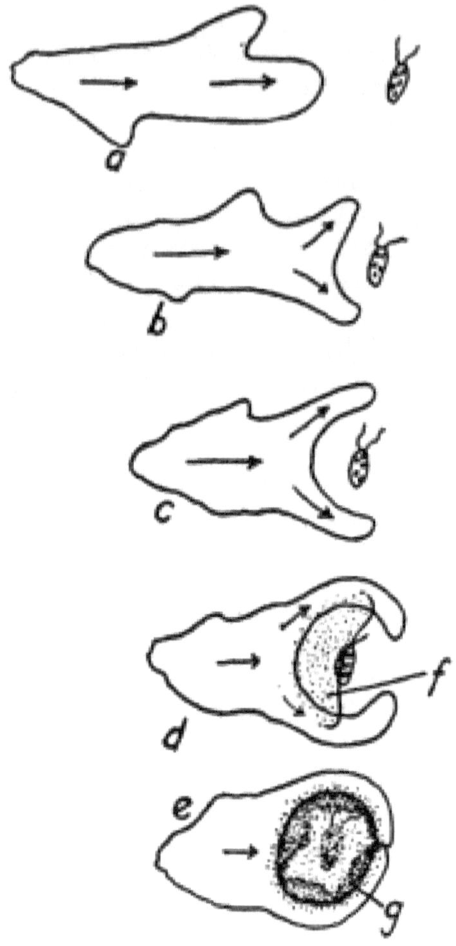

FIGURE 2.

Endoplasmic streaming involved in the formation of a typical food cup. *a*, the ameba is shown moving toward a live food organism that is resting quietly on the bottom. *b*, the main pseudopod forks, being the first indication that the feeding process has set in. At *c* the pseudopods have half-way surrounded the prey, but without having come into contact with it. At *d* the upper sheet of protoplasm, *f*, (stippled), is flowing dome-like over the prey, while the pseudopods continue to surround it. At *e* the pseudopods have met and fused with each other and the upper sheet of protoplasm has completely covered the space encircled by the pseudopods, and has fused with the pseudopods. *g*, sheets of protoplasm which are thrown out along the *lower* surface *under* the prey, to form a floor to the food cup. Up to stage *e* the ameba has

not come into physical contact with the prey, but is just about to
do so. With the completion of the floor of the food cup, the process
of feeding is completed.

At least the same response was produced on the part of the ameba when the ameba was carefully stimulated by means of very fine clean glass needles. The conclusion is unavoidable therefore that the shape of the food cup and the method of its formation is a racial characteristic and is hereditary. The streaming endoplasm therefore, upon suitable stimulation, takes on a definite form, that of a food cup. This indicates again that the endoplasm is something more than the ordinary fluids of physics, for out of an apparently structureless fluid, organization is effected.

The fact that food cups are formed by amebas implies of course that stimuli are received whose effect cannot be explained as a direct physical reaction. Rhumbler ('10) has attempted to explain the formation of food cups as the direct physical result of the stimulation by the food body; but in recent experiments Schaeffer ('16) has shown that food cups are formed over diffusing solutions of tyrosin, where the solutions were quite as concentrated outside as inside the cup. These results prove convincingly that the shape and size of the food cup are not determined by direct action of the stimulating agent, but by hereditary factors within the protoplasm of the ameba.

Other stimuli also affect streaming characteristically, though not so strikingly perhaps as food stimuli. One of the most widely observed effects on streaming is the momentary pause following stimulation of many sorts. If an ameba that is moving along unstimulated externally, suddenly comes near a food object, it frequently stops forward streaming for about a second, and then begins again, usually at increased speed. The ameba behaves as if it were startled. A similar reaction is observed if a small perpendicular beam of light is flashed near the anterior end of the ameba. Here also streaming is resumed with accelerated speed toward the beam of light. Harrington and Leaming ('00) showed that if strong light, especially at the blue end of the spectrum, is suddenly thrown on the ameba, movement is arrested for a short time. Miss Hyman ('17) has shown recently that if an ameba is strongly stimulated with a glass needle, streaming is arrested momentarily, but the direction of streaming when resumed subsequently, depends partly upon the former direction of streaming and partly upon the location of the stimulus. All of these cases of temporarily arrested movement are strikingly similar to what is observed in the higher animals under similar conditions.

The ingestion of a large food mass produces usually a marked change in streaming. A more or less spherical form is assumed, and if the food mass be a live organism such as a large ciliate, the ameba frequently remains quiet for a considerable interval. If a large amount of food is eaten, as for example a dozen or two colpidia, the ameba may suspend concerted streaming for an hour or more. During this time small pseudopods are projected here and there, but there is no locomotion. But if an ameba eats large masses of carmine, there is usually no pause following ingestion, and the same thing is true when the ameba is induced to eat bits of glass and other indigestible substances. It follows therefore that the interrupted streaming of the endoplasm due to feeding is not caused by the act of ingestion as such, but rather by the onset and continuance of the normal digestive processes on a large scale. These reactions are again strikingly similar to what is observed in many vertebrates, in which a more or less definite body sense, whose sense organs are in the splanchnic region, is supposed to be involved; but what the explanation of similar behavior in ameba is, is not at all clear.

Another factor of great importance in endoplasmic streaming is the nucleus. It was observed by Hofer ('90) that amebas lacking nuclei did not move in a coordinated manner. Štolc ('10) however records a number of observations in which characteristic movement was observed in enucleate amebas ten or more days after the enucleate ameba had been cut off from a normal ameba. Hofer's amebas died after nine or ten days, while Štolc's remained alive, some of them for over thirty days. Recently Willis ('16) confirmed Hofer's findings, but does not discuss Štolc's results.

The cutting of an ameba into two pieces, one with and the other without a nucleus, is a very simple operation. It is also very easy to observe that within an hour or so the enucleate ameba does not move normally, and that there is no concerted endoplasmic streaming while the nucleate ameba seems to behave normally. But Štolc's contention that enucleate amebas move characteristically (l. c., p. 159, 160, 167) is not necessarily contradicted by these observations, for Štolc's observations refer to amebas that lived much longer than the enucleate amebas of Hofer and of Willis. Even if an enucleate ameba is able to recover, after many days, its power of concerted movement, there can be no doubt that enucleate amebas do not move characteristically for a short time after the operation, and that this effect is due to the lack of a nucleus.

Very likely the action of the nucleus on the locomotory processes is neither direct nor specific. The metabolic balance must be disturbed by so fundamental an operation as the removal of the nucleus, and all fundamental activities must in consequence be affected. That food organisms (chilomonas and coleps) may be eaten and digested as Štolc ('10) states, indicates however that the metabolic balance may after a time be regained in some degree, for feeding undoubtedly calls for concerted streaming, and digestion for the formation and transfer of enzymes. Until this point receives further attention therefore, it remains unknown in what way the removal of the nucleus disturbs streaming for some time after the operation; but of the fact that streaming is disorganized for some time, there can be no doubt.

CHAPTER IV

THE TRANSFORMATION OF ENDOPLASM INTO ECTOPLASM

Perhaps none of the factors influencing the streaming of the endoplasm mentioned above exercises as profound and constant an influence as its capacity to form ectoplasm. As has been intimated earlier (p. 3-9) streaming as observed during locomotion is not supposed to be possible at all unless accompanied by the formation of ectoplasm at the forward ends of pseudopods, and its transformation into endoplasm at the posterior end of the ameba. We may therefore next consider the rôle ectoplasm plays in locomotion, and in some other fundamental activities of the ameba.

In the first place it is necessary to define the word ectoplasm, for two entirely different meanings are sometimes given to it. It is used often to designate the clear non-granular layer of protoplasm which thinly covers some of the commoner amebas, and is especially prominent in some of the small species, where the larger part of the anterior end often consists of protoplasm quite free from granules. The other use to which the word is put is to designate the layer of protoplasm on or near the outside of the ameba which is more or less rigid and motionless, resembling the gel state of a colloid. It is the latter meaning that is given the word as used in this discussion, while I shall follow Jennings ('04) and other, earlier, writers in using the word hyaloplasm in speaking of the outer clear layer. It may be necessary to add that neither of these two words is strictly definable, for in some cases, at least, hyaloplasm is not more rigid than the endoplasm, while in other cases it is. Strictness of definition can, of course, come only as investigation proceeds; and these words as well as the word endoplasm, should not be taken as defining the properties of the substances to which they refer, but only as labels.

The demonstration of the most conspicuous and important property of ectoplasm in *Amoeba proteus* is easily made. With the high power of the microscope one focusses on the upper surface of an active pseudopod, paying especial attention to the small crystals imbedded in the protoplasm. These crystals, although they dance about slightly (Brownian movement) and otherwise change position to a slight extent, nevertheless appear to be held in place by a very viscous medium. Such movement as is observed in these crystals appears more or less erratic; it is not coordinated and it is only by chance in the direction of locomotion of the ameba. While observing the practically stationary crystals of the ectoplasm one can at the same time, though indistinctly, see the forward sweep of the crystals and other granules in the endoplasm below. But observation fails to detect a definite line of separation between the stationary ectoplasm and the mobile endoplasm; the one grades off insensibly into the other.

The formation of ectoplasm in *proteus* is a much more complicated process than in almost any other ameba, excepting the large species *Amoeba carolinensis*[1] discovered by Wilson ('00). We shall have occasion however to refer at length to the method of ectoplasm formation in *proteus* later on, so we may consider *proteus* first from this point of view, and then take up a few other species in which the process is simpler.

It is a fact more or less familiar to observers of amebas that *proteus*, as distinguished from the other amebas, has a number of large irregular, roughly longitudinal folds or ridges on its pseudopods and on its main body (Figure 3). Under normal conditions these are never absent. They are not found at the free ends of advancing pseudopods, but they take their origin at some little distance from the ends. It is this characteristic of ridge formation that complicates the process of the transformation of endoplasm into ectoplasm; for instead of having to deal with ectoplasm formation at the anterior ends of pseudopods only, we find this process taking place irregularly all over the surface of the ameba.

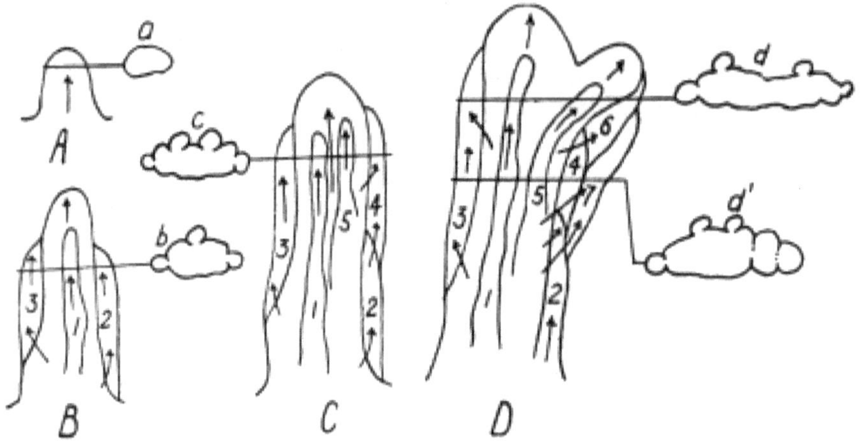

FIGURE 3.

Formation of longitudinal ridges and grooves in the ectoplasm of *Amoeba proteus*. A, B, C, D, showing stages in the development of a single pseudopod. *a, b, c, d, d*[1], cross sections of pseudopods at the levels indicated. The arrows show the direction of endoplasmic streaming with special reference to the formation of ridges. The numerals 1 to 7 indicate the order in which the ridges were formed. Note the tongues of ectoplasm which extend into the en-

---

[1] Wilson ('00) describes it as *Pelomyxa*, but it has much closer affinities with *Amoeba*. It is in fact perhaps the closest relative of *Amoeba proteus*. Ectoplasm formation, and especially the formation of ectoplasmic ridges in *carolinensis*, is exactly like that in *proteus*.

doplasm, in the cross sections.

These folds or ridges were first observed by Leidy ('79) and it is an eloquent tribute to the keen observation of this sympathetically-minded naturalist, that of the large number of subsequent writers on ameboid movement only one (Penard, '02, p. 63) seems to have noticed these folds. Leidy says that " ... the main trunk and larger pseudopods of the same ameba (*proteus*) assumed more or less the appearance of being longitudinally folded. The endosarc axially flowed as if in the interior of thick walled canals, of which the walls appeared to be composed of finer granular matter with scattered imbedded crystals. In the flow, all the contents did not move with the same rapidity, and usually the smaller particles were swept quickly by the larger ones. Other matter, including some of the largest elements appeared to stick to the inner surface of the extemporaneous tubes, but successively became detached to be carried along with the rest of the contents (p. 46)." "The endosarc appeared to flow within thick walls of ectosarc which often seemed to be longitudinally folded (p. 326)." Penard ('02) confirms Leidy's observation as to the existence of these folds: "The current (of endoplasm) indeed is not unified, but there exist many currents at the same time because of the fact that the endosarc is divided into a certain number of longitudinal canals or grooves by dense walls, which are of a temporary nature, being broken down and built up from time to time. It is easy to distinguish one canal from the other in this species, the currents being at first more or less parallel, but terminating at the forward end, by their coalescence, as a single mass of liquid (p. 63)." But Penard questions Leidy's conclusion that the walls are of ectoplasm: "Moreover Leidy deceives himself without any doubt in considering these partitions as folds of the *ectosarc*. The latter, in the rhizopods, is not a special substance, it is a plasma of surface, specialized for the functions which it has to perform, capable of modification as to its intimate structure, but only so temporarily (p. 63)."

Although it is a very simple matter to prove to one's satisfaction the mere existence of these folds—a few minutes' observation under the high power of the microscope will do that—it is a much more difficult matter to observe how these folds originate, because of the incessant changes going on, as recorded by Leidy.

Very young or small pseudopods in *proteus* have the same general appearance as the pseudopods of other large species (*dubia, laureata, discoides, annulata,* etc.); that is, there is a central axial stream of endoplasm surrounded by a layer of ectoplasm. But there is one difference even here, and that is the greater thickness of the ectoplasmic walls in *proteus* in proportion to the diameter of the pseudopod. The ectoplasmic tube however is not solid throughout, but is more or less honeycombed, somewhat like a network, with the spaces filled by endoplasm.

If the ectoplasm is actually endoplasm that has passed into the gel state, then the honeycomb condition just described resembles an intermediate stage where only a part of the endoplasm has been transformed. This network of endoplasm is strong enough however to impede the flow of the main stream of endoplasm along the sides of the pseudopod; but when large objects, such as the nucleus or food masses, too large to be readily carried in the endoplasmic stream, impinge against the imperfectly solidified sides of the tube of ectoplasm, the innermost strands of the spongy network of ectoplasm snap, usually with readiness, allowing the large object to pass by.

The surface of a young pseudopod is smooth, a cross section being oval in shape (Figure 3, *a*); but as the pseudopod increases in size, large folds or ridges begin to make their appearance. Usually the first ridges to appear are lateral. They begin as small waves of hyaloplasm which flow out along the sides of the pseudopod for a short distance and then continue to move forward. The endoplasm then flows in a number of small parallel streams amid numerous obstructions through the ectoplasmic tube of the pseudopod into the wave of ectoplasm. After the ridge is well begun, there is frequently observed a slow forward-moving stream of endoplasm within it, but the ridge is never closed from the main endoplasmic stream, as is readily proved by the numerous small streams of endoplasm which continually filter through the ectoplasm into the ridge.

In addition to the lateral ridges, which, as stated, are usually formed first, there appear ridges on the upper side of the pseudopod as well, and presumably also on the under side. So far as could be determined these ridges are all formed in much the same way; that is, by the projection of a small wave of protoplasm from some part of the surface of the pseudopod. The ridges do not always grow by extension at the anterior end as described above. Not infrequently a ridge ten to twenty times as long as wide is pushed out along its whole length at once. This is especially likely to happen in a slender pseudopod that suddenly becomes the main pseudopod. The width of a ridge, especially on the upper surface, does not change much after formation. One can frequently find two or three ridges of about the same width, which run the whole length of the ameba with the exception of a short distance at the anterior end, where, as before stated, there are no ridges.

As the figure indicates, new ridges may be formed from previous ones, either by lateral or endwise extension. In such case the walls of the ridge send out thin waves of hyaloplasm followed by streams of endoplasm, as described above in the formation of the first ridge on a pseudopod. When a pseudopod forms a branch, the ridges on the old pseudopod do not likewise branch, but new ridges are formed which have no connection with old ones, but they may later coalesce with old ridges. Such coalescence is however exceptional. Once a ridge is formed, it retains its identity as a rule; that is, as the ameba moves forward, the ridge in effect moves back over the ameba to lose itself in the wrinkles at the posterior end (See Figure 11, *A*). The number of ridges on any random selection of amebas is variable, and is moreover difficult to state. A large ameba may have as many as six or seven side by side on its upper surface. The number on the sides and on the lower surface are difficult to estimate. The space between ridges is about equal to the width of the ridges, but as one passes toward the posterior end, the ridges become more closely crowded together.

From these observations on the formation of ridges it is evident that they do not represent a wrinkling of the surface such as occurs in a semi-rigid curved surface when it is made to occupy a smaller space. The ridges are wrinkles only in appearance, not in origin. The surface of the ridges is younger than the space between them. It appears as if the pseudopod which has to widen as it increases in length, could not liquify the ectoplasm uniformly all around, but only in longitudinal strips here and there, and that through these openings the ectoplasm then flows. There is no question about the greater readiness with which ectoplasm is formed in this ameba as compared with many others, but after a careful comparison of *proteus* and *carolinensis*, where ridges are formed, with *discoides* (Figure 11, B), *dubia* (Figure 11, C), *laureata* (Figure 4) and *annulata*, where none are formed, the only conclusion presenting itself is that the visible physical properties of the protoplasm of *proteus* and *carolinensis* give no hint as to the cause of the presence of ridges in these species. The protoplasm of *discoides* and *laureata* is about as viscous as that of *proteus*, yet in these there is never any ridge formation.

The ridges in *proteus* recall, of course, the ridges always observed in *verrucosa*, *sphaeronucleosus* (Figure 13) and their congeners, especially while the latter are in locomotion. A *sphaeronucleosus* is especially favorable for study in this connection because of its greater activity. This ameba has four or more longitudinal ridges on its upper surface, while in locomotion, which strongly resemble those in *proteus* and *carolinensis*. The chief difference lies in the fact that in *sphaeronucleosus* the ridges are extended at their anterior ends continually, and unless the direction of locomotion is changed, the ridges may retain their identity while the ameba moves several scores of times the length of its body. Along the sides, however, new ridges are continually replacing older ones. When the direction of locomotion is changed, the old ridges usually all disappear into a jumble of ridges and crinkles running in every conceivable direction, and with the reestablishment of locomotion along a more or less straight path, a new set of ridges appears. In *sphaeronucleosus* and its congeners, the ridges are also not wrinkles, but ridges that are formed later than the surface contiguous to them.

It is interesting to recall also that the ectoplasm in *sphaeronucleosus*, *verrucosa* and the rest of this group, is much firmer than in most other amebas.

CHAPTER V

PSEUDOPODS AND THE NATURE OF THE ECTO-PLASM

In contrast with the ridge-forming amebas stand those with smooth ectoplasm, such as the common *dubia, discoides, villosa,* and the rarer *laureata* and *annulata,* to mention only a few of the larger forms. In addition to these may be mentioned all the pelomyxas and nearly all the smaller amebas. Much the larger number of species of amebas do not form ridges in the ectoplasm during locomotion.

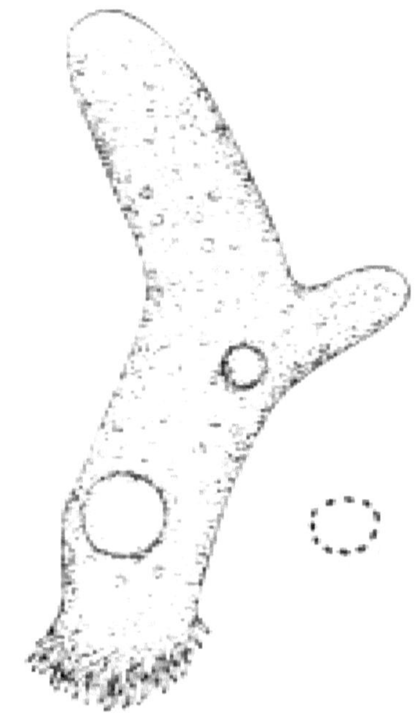

FIGURE 4.

Amoeba laureata. This ameba is multinucleate, containing a thousand or more nuclei of the shape shown at the right. Ameba 1000 microns long in locomotion. Nuclei 10 microns in diameter.

Of all the amebas with smooth surfaces, the most favorable for observation as to the formation of ectoplasm, is the giant *laureata* (Figure 4), though it is unfortunately of infrequent occurrence. This species is as often found in clavate form as with pseudopods. In cross section it is circular or nearly so. It is often found with *zoochlorella* growing in it, upon which it seems to depend largely for food, for it seldom has distinctive food masses in it. The nuclei are small and very numerous and the crystals are well formed and numerous, each in a small vacuole, and of a size about two or three times those found in *proteus*. It will be seen therefore that there are only small bodies in this ameba, none of which (excepting the contractile vacuole) are large enough to change the course of the endoplasmic stream, and streaming is thus reduced to what might be called a typical condition.

In this ameba the endoplasmic stream flows uniformly towards the anterior end where it spreads out slightly so as to preserve the same general diameter of the ameba, for it is a characteristic of this ameba that the anterior end is of about the same diameter as the posterior, when in clavate form. The ectoplasmic tube is built at the anterior end, and remains as constructed until it is drawn in at the posterior end to form endoplasm. It is not all the time undergoing changes such as are observed in *proteus*. This characteristic is very well shown by focusing with the high power of the microscope on the upper surface of the ameba. The immobility of the ectoplasm is much more readily observed in *laureata* than in perhaps any other species, a condition that is due chiefly to the large crystals whose displacement is the most convenient criterion of ectoplasmic mobility.

The ectoplasmic tube is not as thick as in *proteus*, though it appears to be more solid than in that species. It is thrown into folds at the posterior end as it is liquified to form endoplasm, which indicates a firm texture of the ectoplasm. As to the endoplasmic stream, it presents no visible characteristics which set it apart from the fluids of physics; it moves most rapidly in the middle, and gradually less rapidly as the ectoplasm is approached. There is no backward movement of the ectoplasm against the sides of the pseudopod at the anterior end—nothing approaching a "fountain current"—which indicates that the transformation of endoplasm into ectoplasm is rapid and complete. That is, all the endoplasm which reaches the anterior end is turned into ectoplasm. Typically this would result in an ameba of average size, in a layer of ectoplasm of a thickness of about one-seventh of the diameter of the pseudopod (for the area of the cut ectoplasmic tube would equal the area of the endoplasmic stream). But because of friction against the sides of the ectoplasmic tube, there is a layer of endoplasm of appreciable thickness that is practically motionless. This layer of endoplasm therefore makes the diameter of the endoplasmic stream appear smaller than it actually is, and the ectoplasmic tube larger than it is. The actual thickness of the tube of ectoplasm, as distinguished from the flowing endoplasm, is difficult to measure, but it seems to be about one-tenth the diameter of the pseudopod. (Kite ('13) found ameboid ectoplasm to be from eight to twelve microns thick, but he does not state from what part of the ameba nor from what species the ectoplasm was taken.) This would indicate that if the transformation of endoplasm into ectoplasm is as complete as the conditions permit, the thickness of the friction layer would be about one-twenty-third of the diameter of the pseudopod. These observations therefore point to the conclusion that the tendency in *laureata* is for all the endoplasm to be transformed into ectoplasm at the anterior end, and for the reverse process to occur at the posterior end.

Several of the pelomyxas also move in much the same manner as *Amoeba laureata*, that is, in clavate form and more or less cylindrical in shape. This is especially the case with *Pelomyxa palustris* and *P. belevskii*. But in these species the endoplasm is not completely converted into ectoplasm at the anterior end, as is shown by the fact that there is a slight backward current of endoplasm at the sides near the anterior end (Schultze, '75). Observation indicates also that the ectoplasmic tube is thinner than would be the case were there complete transformation of endoplasm into ectoplasm at the anterior end. The origin of pseudopods in these pelomyxas is not steady and under control as in *laureata*, but sudden and eruptive, indicating a less coherent ectoplasm.

The nearest approach to the conditions of streaming as found in *Amoeba laureata* is found in *A. discoides* (Figure 11, *B*) a species often confounded with *proteus*. This species is frequently found in clavate form, and the conversion of endoplasm into ectoplasm is complete at the anterior end. In other respects of streaming and pseudopod formation, the two species are also similar.

In another very common species of ameba, *Amoeba dubia* (Figure 11, *C*) the clavate stage of locomotion is comparatively rare, but when it is found it is observed that the transformation of endoplasm into ectoplasm at the anterior end is incomplete, and the endoplasm seems to be of very liquid consistency. This ameba is characterized by the possession, usually, of numerous pseudopods extending from a central mass of protoplasm. In this stage it possesses no *main* pseudopod as does *proteus*, *discoides*, *laureata* and other species, but there are three or four pseudopods extending actively in the general direction of locomotion. The physical characteristics of these pseudopods, in so far as streaming is affected, are different from those of the clavate amebas. The ectoplasmic tubes are relatively thicker, the endoplasm is less fluid, and new pseudopods are not formed so readily. It appears therefore that an increase of surface in the ameba serves to increase the amount of ectoplasm that is formed during locomotion.

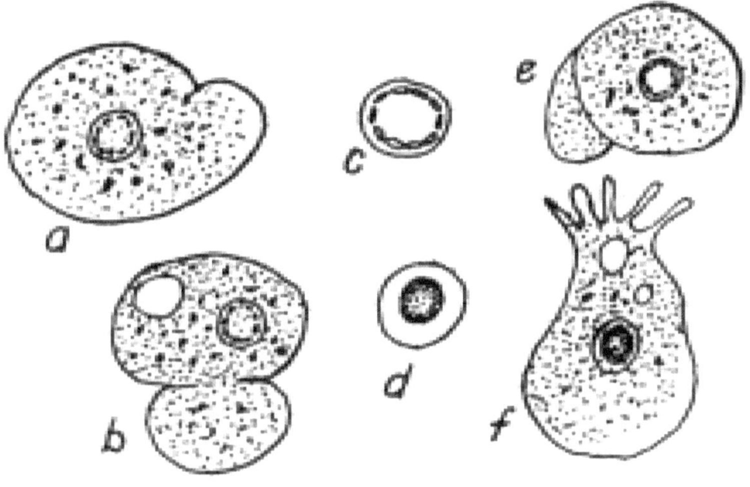

FIGURE 5.

Amoeba limicola, after Penard. Figures *a, b, e,* illustrate the "eruptive pseudopods" by means of which this ameba moves. *f,* a variety or separate species whose ectoplasm is somewhat firmer, and
whose posterior end possesses a conspicuous uroid. *c,* the nucleus
found in *a, b, e. d,* the nucleus found in *f.*

There is another group of amebas in which the endoplasm is much more fluid
than in *dubia.* To this group belong *Amoeba limicola* (Figure 5) and *Pelomyxa schiedti*
(Figure 6). The latter never forms pseudopods, and the former does so very seldom. *A. limicola* is extremely fluid, and in locomotion the flow of the endoplasm
can hardly be called streaming, for it rushes about in the body as if it were only
partially under control. The ectoplasm does not give way steadily at the anterior
end during locomotion, allowing a steady forward flow of the endoplasm, but it
breaks away suddenly here or there, allowing the endoplasm to rush through as
if it were under considerable pressure. When the endoplasm rushes through these
breaches in the ectoplasm, it is usually deflected back along the side of the ameba
for a considerable distance, thus leaving a part of the old ectoplasmic wall stand
for a few seconds between the reflected wave of ectoplasm and the main body of
the ameba. It is then that one can observe especially well the very thin ectoplasm
covering the ameba, the thickness of which is about one-fortieth the diameter of
the ameba. This ameba is somewhat dorso-ventrally flattened and generally ob-
long in shape during locomotion.

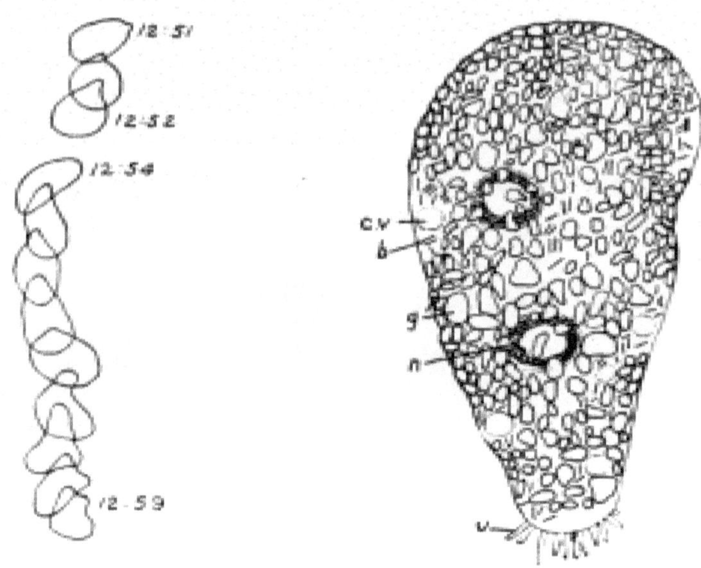

FIGURE 6.

Pelomyxa schiedti, after Schaeffer. *b*, bacterial rods characteristic of
the genus *Pelomyxa*. *c, v*, contractile vacuole. *g*, glycogen bodies. *n*,
nucleus. *u*, uroidal projections. At the left is shown a series of outlines of the animal during locomotion. Length, about 75 microns.

Pelomyxa schiedti moves in much the same way that *Amoeba limicola* does; that
is, by eruptive waves of endoplasm which are usually deflected back along the
side (Figure 6, at the left). The endoplasm is likewise of very thin consistency. The
thinness of the ectoplasm and the ease with which it may be ruptured, is very well
shown by the fact that the large irregular glycogen bodies (Štolc, '00) which fill
it to capacity, lie so close to the surface that it is frequently impossible to see any
protoplasm between them and the exterior. The contractile vacuoles which are
numerous, also testify in their characteristics, to the ease with which the ectoplasm
may be broken. The vacuoles never reach but a very small size (four microns in diameter) presumably because of the thin consistency of the endoplasm and because
they can readily break through the ectoplasm. They burst on the surface of the
ameba instantaneously, as a small air bubble might burst on pure water. But this
ameba differs from *limicola* in that a cross section of the body is very nearly a circle.

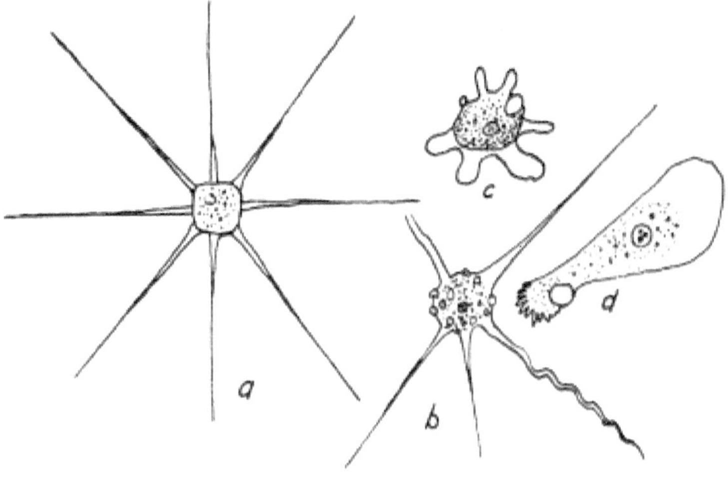

FIGURE 7.

Amoeba radiosa, after Penard. *a*, the rayed stage. *b*, the rayed stage in which some of the pseudopods are being withdrawn. One of them is thrown into a spiral as it is being withdrawn. *c*, the stage preceding the trophic stage shown at *d*.

Another very interesting feature of *Pelomyxa schiedti* is the uroid (Figure 6, *u*), which in this species consists of a number of very thin projections resembling pseudopods extending from the posterior end. These projections are attached to the substratum and in some way aid in locomotion. These uroidal projections are of considerable length, and may persist for a considerable length of time. Thus while *schiedti* is unable to form pseudopods at its anterior end, it forms uroidal projections with great ease at its posterior end. But what the conditions are which are necessary for the formation of a uroid, a structure which it may be added, exists in many species of amebas (and perhaps also in Cercomonas), is quite unknown.

In contrast to the amebas thus far discussed from the point of view of the transformation of endoplasm into ectoplasm, there are a number of species in which two distinct methods of endoplasmic transformation occur typically. Among these species are the small *Amoeba radiosa* (Figure 7), *A. bigemma* (Figure 8) and a new species which for convenience will be referred to as *bilzi*.

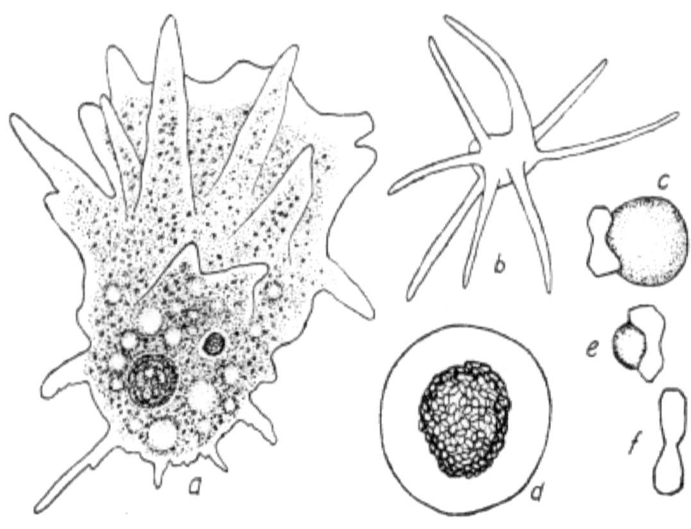

FIGURE 8.

Amoeba bigemma, after Schaeffer. *a,* usual form in locomotion, showing the numerous pseudopods, vacuoles, nucleus and food body. *b,* rayed stage frequently assumed when suspended in the water. The pseudopods in this stage are clear, slender, and more rigid than those in stage *a. c,* an excretion sphere attached to a twin-crystal characteristic of this ameba. *d,* the nucleus, consisting of a clear nuclear membrane and a mass of chromatin granules in the center. *e,* a small sphere attached to a crystal. *f,* a twin crystal unattached to a sphere. Length of *a,* 150 microns; of *d,* 12 microns; of *f,* 2 microns.

It is well known that *radiosa* has two stages: a more or less clavate shaped stage in which the ameba creeps along the surface of some object (Figure 7, *d*); and a stage in which a number (eight or less) of long and very slender tapering pseudopods are formed which usually persist for a long time (Figure 7, *a, b*). These pseudopods are frequently quite straight and regularly disposed around the central mass of protoplasm (Penard, '02, pp. 87, 89). In no case are any endoplasmic granules found in these slender pseudopods; they consist entirely of hyaloplasm. In retracting these pseudopods a curious phenomenon is sometimes observed; the pseudopod is rolled up into several (as many as six) turns of an almost perfect helical spiral of a diameter six to eight times that of the pseudopod. But as the process of withdrawal proceeds, the spiral becomes irregular, but parts of some of the turns persist in the last vestiges preceding complete withdrawal (Figure 7, *b*). These spirals are also observed in other species besides *radiosa* (see p. 128 seq.)

Another species of ameba in which a trophic as well as a rayed stage is found, is the recently described species *bigemma*. In this species the rayed stage is only of occasional occurrence (Figure 8, *b*). The larger the ameba is, the rarer is the rayed stage assumed. On very rare occasions one finds a rayed stage in which the pseudopods are long, straight, slender and tapering, and more or less regularly disposed around the central mass of protoplasm. The trophic stage (Figure 8, *a*) is much the more common. In this condition pseudopods are formed in large number. They are small, conical or linear, and blunt, and they do not determine the direction of locomotion, as they do in *proteus, dubia,* or *laureata.* These pseudopods are often composed only of hyaloplasm, though frequently the basal parts of them consist of endoplasm. When these amebas become suspended in the water, they frequently assume a shape that approaches the rayed condition: six or more long conical pseudopods are run out from the central mass of protoplasm, but the pseudopods are not straight in this case, but irregularly curved and capable of being waved about to a slight extent. The ameba readily passes from this stage to the trophic.

The species *Amoeba bilzi* (Figure 9) has come under my observation on several occasions, and its pseudopodial characters are of considerable interest in this connection. In its usual form this ameba has the general appearance of a *sphaeronucleosus.*

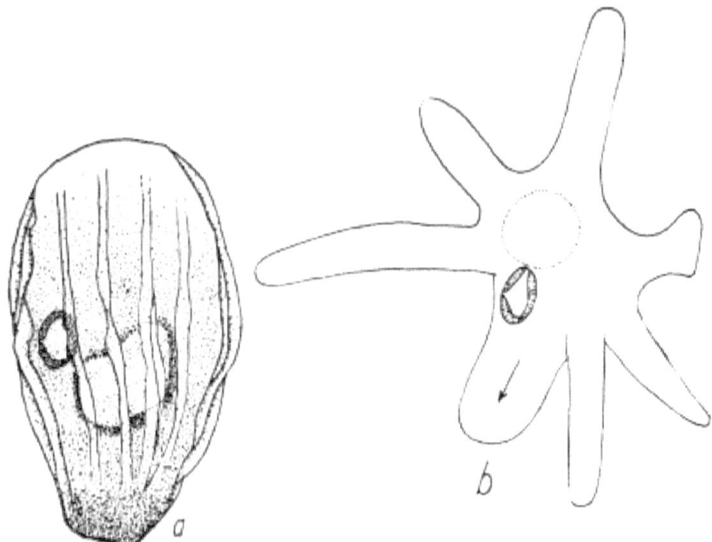

FIGURE 9.

Amoeba bilzi. a, the ameba in locomotion, showing the ectoplasmic ridges, nucleus, contractile vacuole. *b,* the transition stage between the rayed stage (which resembles that of *radiosa,* Figure 5, p. 30, somewhat) and the stage shown at *a.* The whole of the ameba flows into the broad pseudopod with the arrow. Length of *a,* 90 microns.

In size it is about midway between the latter species and *striata.* It always has a number of prominent longitudinal ridges on its upper surface. Its mode of streaming is essentially like that of *striata* or *sphaeronucleosus*. When this ameba is disturbed and left suspended in the water, it throws out four or five or more long slender pseudopods composed entirely of hyaloplasm, excepting a bulbous base which consists of granular endoplasm. The pseudopods are cylindrical with tapering ends. They are very rigid, and once formed, persist for a considerable length of time. When these pseudopods are about to be retracted, the wall weakens at some point and then crinkles while the distal part of the pseudopod bends, often at a decided angle. The crinkling of the wall continues up and down the pseudopod while it is slowly being withdrawn. These pseudopods, as well as those of the rayed state in *radiosa* and *bigemma*, are not pseudopods of locomotion but of *position*; they are not dynamic but static structures. But there are no hard and fast distinctions to be made between these two types of pseudopods, for at least in *bigemma* and *bilzi*, there are transitional forms of pseudopods (Figure 8, *b*).

The formation of pseudopods and their character depends to some extent upon the firmness and thickness of the ectoplasmic layer; and the character of the ectoplasm in turn depends largely upon the consistency of the protoplasm as a whole. In the following representative list of amebas: *limicola, villosa, dubia, proteus, discoides, laureata, bigemma, bilzi, radiosa, sphaeronucleosus, verrucosa*, the given order indicates a progressively thicker and firmer ectoplasm as one passes from *limicola* to *verrucosa*. But from *limicola* to *bilzi* the number of pseudopods directing locomotion increases from one to an average of about twelve in *dubia*, and then falls gradually to one in *bilzi* and the others beyond in the list. (See Figure 10.) Where the directive pseudopods begin to disappear, the transitional appear, viz., in *bigemma* and *bilzi*; but beyond these no transitional pseudopods occur. But along with the transitional there begin to appear also the static pseudopods, which are seen relatively seldom in *bigemma* and *bilzi* while in *radiosa* they occur at almost all times. In *sphaeronucleosus* and *verrucosa* no distinctive pseudopods of any kind occur.

If all the known species of amebas in which the necessary characteristics have been recorded, were arranged similarly with respect to the firmness and the thickness of the ectoplasm, the general relations of the various kinds of pseudopods in the list would be approximately the same as in the list given above; but there would appear an exception here and there, indicating the operation of special factors. Such an exception, for example, is seen in *proteus* in the list of species given, which because of the ridges that it forms (Figure 3) has a smaller number of pseudopods than would be the case if no ridges were formed[2]. It may be concluded, then, that the number and character of pseudopods depends in large part upon the ectoplasm-forming capacity of the ameba; and that this property is intimately associated with the degree of fluidity of the whole mass of protoplasm in the ameba.

---

[2] This is shown by the fact that after this ameba has taken on a spherical shape due to some disturbance in the water, the number of small ridgeless pseudopods thrown out upon resuming movement, is about the same as in *dubia*; but after ridges begin to form, the number of pseudopods decreases.

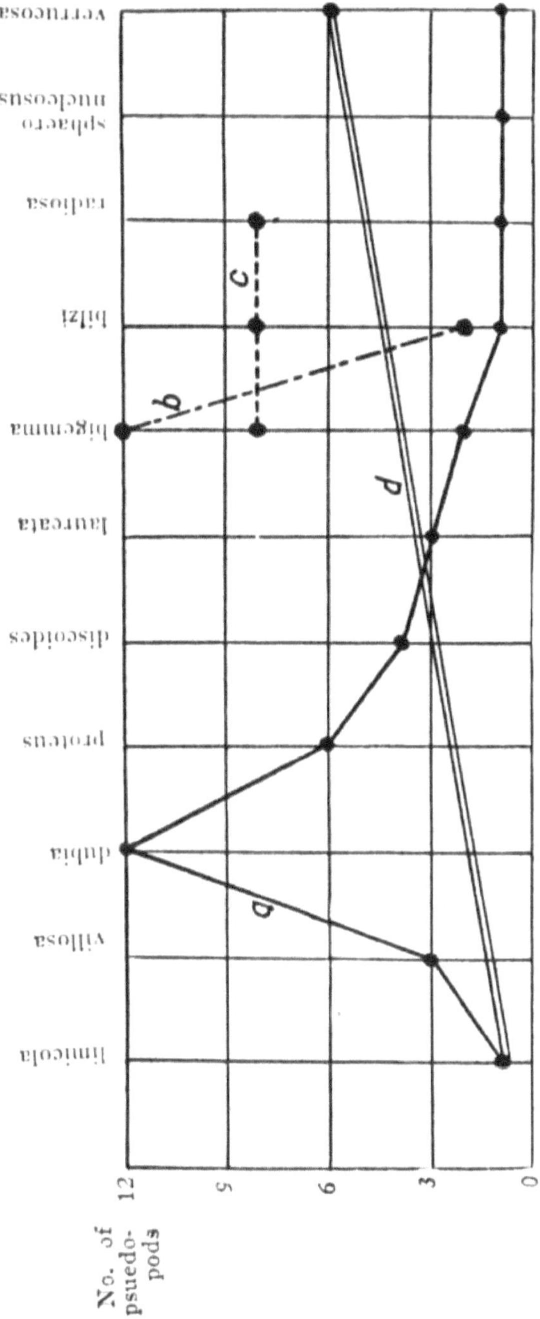

FIGURE 10.

Graph representing the relation of firmness and thickness of the ectoplasm with the number and character of the pseudopods in different species of amebas. *a*, the average maximum number of pseudopods directing locomotion in the different species of amebas. *b*, the number of transitional pseudopods. *c*, the number of static pseudopods. *d*, the estimated degree of firmness and thickness of the ectoplasm of the various species of amebas, grading that of *limicola* as 1 and that of *verrucosa* as 6.

That the number and character of pseudopods formed depends *in large part* upon the firmness and thickness of the ectoplasm was said advisedly. For observations indicate that there are other factors which influence the character of pseudopods besides those which also control the formation of ectoplasm. These other factors indicate their presence readily in the details of structure of the pseudopods. Thus the number of directive, transitional or static pseudopods may be the same in two particular species, yet in their intimate structure and appearance they are always found to differ. In *bigemma*, *bilzi* and *radiosa*, for example, the number of static pseudopods when formed is about the same in the three species, but the similarity ends there. For these species differ in the frequency with which pseudopods are formed, in their persistence when once formed, in the ratio of length to average diameter, in the general shape, in the frequency with which straight pseudopods are formed, in the speed of their formation and withdrawal, in the manner of their withdrawal, in their disposition with respect to geometrical pattern, in the character of the bases of the pseudopods, in the form of the free ends, and so on. Many of these characteristics are still further analyzable into numerous other and more detailed characters. And what is true of the static pseudopods is likewise true of the transitional and the directive. Pseudopod formation is however only a small part of the activity of an ameba. The formation of uroidal projections, of vacuoles of various sorts, of crystals, and so on, are some other general activities that are fully as subject to specific variation as pseudopod formation. Again in behavior to food and various other stimuli, in resistance to various factors in the environment, in reproductive processes, and so forth, there is found similar specific peculiarity. In fact, one looks in vain for similarity between any two species of amebas except in their most generalized characters. From my own experience in extended observation of several dozen species, which included a large number of characters, as pointed out above, I have not found two species of which I can confidently assert that any particular character defined as accurately as possible was present in both. In different words, my experience indicates that no two species are alike in any respect whatsoever. Each species appears unique from every point of view and in the smallest definable detail. The concept of specificity therefore is much more fundamental in amebas than has been believed to be the case hitherto (cf. Calkins, '12). The intimate structure of amebas is indeed similar to that of higher animals where the precipitin reactions (Richet, '02, '12; Reichert and Brown, '09; Dale, '12; Nuttal, '04; also Todd, '14) have indicated that the various albumins are of specific structure and reaction.

As an example of these specific differences, reference may be made to the three species, *protus*, *dubia* and *discoides*, which have been referred to in the past, almost without exception, by the most experienced teachers of biology, as being one species: *proteus*. Some investigators of ameboid phenomena have likewise confused these different amebas. Below is given a list of some of the most striking characteristics of these three amebas. This list is of course very sketchy. If the nuclear division phenomena, for example, were well known, which they are not, those character differences alone would doubtless make a list several times as long as this one. Compare with Figure 11.

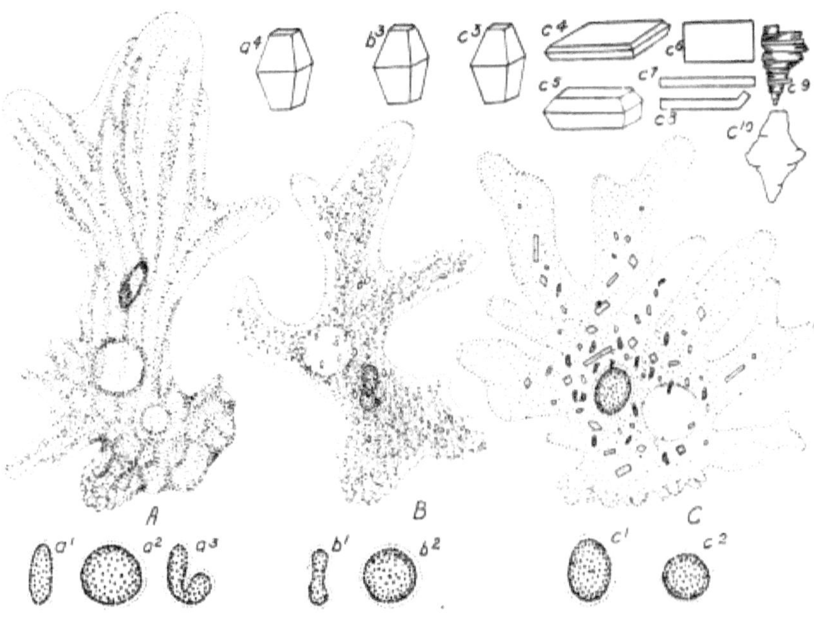

FIGURE 11.

A, Amoeba proteus in locomotion. Note especially the longitudinal ridges. a^1, equatorial view of the *discoid* nucleus. a^2, a polar view of the nucleus. a^3, equatorial view of a folded or crushed nucleus frequently found in large individuals. a^4, shape of crystals found in this species.*B, Amoeba discoides* in locomotion. b^1, b^2, equatorial and polar views of the *discoid* nucleus. b^3, shape of the crystals found in the ameba. *C, Amoeba dubia* in locomotion. c^1 and c^2, equatorial and polar views of the *ovoid* nucleus. c^3-c^{10}, shapes of crystals found in *dubia*. In these drawings only such characters as are of special interest for the purpose of this work are emphasized. Dimensions in microns: *A*, 600; *B*, 450; *C*, 400; a^1, 46 × 12; b^1, 40 × 18; c^1, 40 × 32; a^4, maximum, 4.5; b^3, maximum, 2.5; c^3-c^{10}, maxima, 10 to 30.

This fundamental uniqueness of all the characters of the various species of amebas naturally gives rise to the question as to what is the cause of this condition of affairs. Why and how are the different species of amebas so absolutely different, even to the smallest detail? Why are the apparent resemblances and similarities of their more generalized kinetic characters, such as the formation of pseudopods, of ectoplasm, of crystals, of contractile vacuoles, the general character of endoplasmic streaming, the formation of ectoplasmic ridges, and so forth, found, upon analysis, to resolve themselves into a large number of details which differ more strikingly, the corresponding characters of one from those of the other, than do the generalized characters of which they are composed?

Characteristics	*Amoeba discoides*	*Amoeba proteus*	*Amoeba dubia*
Size in locomotion	450 microns	600 microns	400 microns
Pseudopods	cylindrical smooth ectoplasm "main" pseudopod present cross section circular average number in locomotion, three	dorso-ventrally flattened ectoplasm "main" pseudopod present cross section an irregular oval average number in locomotion, five	dorso-ventrally flattened smooth ectoplasm no "main" pseudopod cross section oval average number in locomotion, twelve
Crystals	very numerous all uniform truncated bi-pyramids maximum size 2.5μ	less than in *discoides* all uniform truncated bi-pyramids; rarely a few flat plates maximum size 4.5μ	relatively few at least four varieties present; few perfect crystals maximum size 10μ, 12μ, 30μ
Fission	slower than *proteus*	average 1 division in 48 hours at 20° C.	faster than *proteus*
Maximum time between divisions	20 days	8 days	6 days
Multinuclearity	binucleate occasionally	binucleate frequent; tetranucleate occasional	binucleate very rarely
Nucleus, shape	biconcave disc, never folded	biconcave disc, frequently folded	ovoidal
Size	40μ × 18μ	46μ × 12μ	40μ × 32μ
General resistance to same conditions	slight	very great	greater than *discoides*
Surface of posterior end	free from debris	free from debris	carries debris

Effect of mechanical stimuli	slightly responsive	responsive	very responsive
Food cups	small	large	often enormous
Reaction to carmine	readily eaten; rejected in a few minutes	readily eaten; rejected in a few minutes	eaten only occasionally; often retained for hrs.
Distribution	sporadic, small numbers	very common	sporadic, frequently in large numbers

These questions apply, of course, to all other organisms as well as to amebas. Unfortunately, however, these questions are at present unanswerable for all organisms. But for the amebas, at least, the problem of form can be rid of some irrelevant matter which, in numerous instances in the past, has been assumed to be properly included.

In the first place, changing a single character of the protoplasm, such as the degree of viscosity, cannot explain the observed diversity of detail; neither can a variation of a number of the physical characters of fluids produce such differences as are observed in the dynamics of the different species of amebas. Our whole experience with the fluids of physics speaks against such an explanation. But, on the other hand, the invisible details of structure of a fluid may become strikingly manifest under certain conditions, namely, those surrounding the process of crystallization. A slight change in the physical condition may produce a considerable variety of crystal shapes, but this variety of shape has nevertheless very definite limits which cannot be overstepped.

Amebas like crystals are also most rigidly and definitely restricted to a certain range of shape, which must be a direct result of the structure of the protoplasm composing them. Amebas in fact are not any more "shapeless" than crystals are; and it would be quite as exact to say that the crystals of water are shapeless since a great variety of shapes are met with in snow, hoar-frost, etc. The fact that corresponding parts of two species of amebas resemble each other less and less closely as they are analyzed into smaller and smaller details, is in itself conclusive evidence that the protoplasms of the amebas are *chemically* different; the resemblance between the gross anatomy and physiology between two different species is due to the greater conspicuousness of such characters as are the result of the action of physical processes. That is to say, chemically or molecularly different masses of matter may resemble each other in their molar aspects.

It is to be noted however that the more intimate structure of streaming protoplasm cannot always express itself externally as it can in ameba. As was suggested in the introduction, there is no good reason for supposing that the causes of streaming in the various organisms in which it is observed are fundamentally different. The problem of ameboid movement cannot be considered apart from the streaming of protoplasm in foraminifera, myxomycetes, plant cells, lymphocytes, desmids, diatoms and ciliates. The streaming of endoplasm in some cells, such as in ciliates and plant cells, does not give rise to change of shape of the cell as it does in ameba. In these cases the character of streaming is highly restricted; the unyielding ectoplasm or cell wall as the case may be, prevents any but the most essential features of streaming from occurring. Recalling the analogy of crystallization, streaming in a plant cell or in a ciliate is analogous to crystallization occurring in a tube or vessel too small for the crystals to form properly.

This discussion anent the fundamental chemical uniqueness of each species of ameba is of course not complete without an examination of the views expressed to the contrary. And it is to this side of the discussion that we may now briefly direct our attention.

CHAPTER VI
THE SPECIES QUESTION

After the discovery of the ameba by Rösel v. Rosenhof and the introduction of the Linnean system of nomenclature, the number of new species of amebas that were reported increased rapidly. But in 1856 Carter suggested that what had been described as *A. radiosa* probably was a young stage of *A. proteus*. With the general acceptance of the Darwinian Natural Selection Hypothesis, the ameba came to be looked upon as standing at the bottom of the scale of organisms, and consequently was supposed to lack generally such characters as the higher forms possessed. The ameba became the representative of the "primordial slime" from which by slow stages the other organisms were evolved. So of the sixty odd species which had been described up to Leidy's ('79) time, Leidy, following the suggestion of Carter, was inclined to think that the great majority of these represented only changes of shape of about four species (not including the several species that were then known to be parasitic). Since Leidy's time the prevailing tendency has been to regard most of the "new" species as mere environmental or life cycle stages of a very few species. A very noted exception to this tendency, however, has been Penard's ('02) great work on the amebas and other rhizopods of the Leman Basin, in which he describes forty-five species of amebas (including *Gloidium, Protamoeba, Amoeba, Dinamoeba, Pelomyxa*), paying attention mainly to the readily observed ectoplasmic and endoplasmic characters, and the appearance of the resting nucleus.

The remarkable discoveries of Vahlkampf ('05) of the nuclear changes during the division process turned the attention of numerous investigators to this field, and the ectoplasmic and endoplasmic characters thenceforward received scant attention. Thus Calkins ('04) came to suggest as Carter had done many years before, that *A. radiosa* was merely a young form of *A. proteus*. And Doflein ('07) intimated that the protoplasmic characters of *vespertilio* cannot be distinguished from those of *verrucosa, radiosa, polypodia, limax* and *guttula*. Schepotieff ('10) in a similar vein, writes: "Wir werden demnach so bekannte und so lange Zeit als selbstständige und typische Amöbenarten aufgefasste Formen wie *A. limax, A. polypodia,* und *A. radiosa* nur als Umwandlungsstadien andrer Arten bezeichnen dürfen." Gläser ('12) remarks: "The most reliable criterion for the classification of the amebas is the division of the nucleus." Calkins ('12) takes the same view on this point and states that in his opinion the ectoplasmic and endoplasmic characters of amebas conform to four "types," viz., *proteus, verrucosa, vespertilio* and *limax*. The enormous amount of work that has been done on the nuclear division changes as compared with the small amount of work on the cytoplasmic structure has thus naturally tended to an over-estimation of the significance of the nuclear changes.

There are objections to making the nuclear changes the basis of the classification of the amebas.

1. In the first place, to classify the amebas means not only labeling the different species accurately, but also to assign to them their proper place in the system of organisms. All organisms are classified with this purpose in view. This is what is meant by a *natural system of* classification as contrasted with an *artificial system* based on only a part, arbitrarily selected, of each of the organisms concerned. In the past all artificial systems have been discarded. It is perhaps unnecessary to say that a classification based on nuclear characters would be a highly artificial system. For in no group of organisms has it been found possible thus far to use the nuclear changes as a basis of classification. The great amount of labor that has been expended by cytologists within recent years on the behavior of chromosomes, and the immense amount of work done by the students of genetics, has failed to show any specific relation whatever between the external characters of organisms and the nuclear behavior.[3] In other words, the peculiarities of mitotic processes have not been found to be correlated with characters in the somatoplasm. It is to be remembered however that all living organisms, with the exception of some of the bacteria, are classified with respect to their external characters, and that in almost all organisms the number of visible and demonstrable specific characters becomes rapidly greater as ontogenetic development proceeds.

2. There is considerable disagreement among the investigators of the nuclear phenomena of amebas as to the actual events occurring during the division process. Cf. Dobell ('14) and Hartmann ('14) *in re Amoeba lacertae*; Nägler ('09), Gläser ('12) and Wilson ('16) on the presence of a centriole in amebas; etc. The work of Schardinger ('99), Wherry ('13) and Wilson ('16) on the nuclear stages of amebas was done with care, yet Wilson ('16) still remains in doubt as to whether or not these investigators all worked on the same species.

3. Awerinzew ('04, '06) found that the nuclear changes in *Amoeba proteus* are similar to those in the heliozoan *Actinosphaerium*; there being thus greater correspondence in the nuclear changes between species belonging to different orders than there is between species in the same genus. Logically therefore *Actinosphaerium* would have to be placed in the same genus with *Amoeba proteus*.

4. There is the great practical objection that in many of the larger species it is extremely difficult to find suitable division stages even though thousands of individuals are at hand, and the search is continued for days and weeks by an experienced investigator (Dobell, '10). Experimental work, which is usually done with one of the larger species, would thus be greatly handicapped because of the great difficulty in determining the nature of the organism employed.

---

[3] That is, resemblances in nuclear division stages are not correlated with corresponding degrees of resemblance in somatic characters. It is not generally held that the shape or size or number of chromosomes is correlated with any external characters. It is the presence of hypothetical factors or genes which are held to be correlated with somatic characters and their number or arrangement in a chromosome is not in any way related to their character.

From these considerations it appears that the attempt to classify the amebas on the basis of the nuclear changes is highly artificial and exceptional, and if we may judge from past attempts to classify organisms on the basis of a single character, is foredoomed to failure. This conclusion does not apply, however, to very minute amebas in which no specific cytoplasmic characters have yet been established, chiefly because of their very minuteness; such amebas could be given specific names for reference but they could not be classified in a natural system excepting perhaps as a group.

But the definiteness and the consistency with which the nuclear division stages occur in any given species of ameba, lends support to the probability that in these animals the relation existing between the chromatin and the cytoplasm are similar to those observed in higher animals; and that the laws governing the transmission of cytoplasmic characters in amebas are quite as inflexible as those governing somatoplasmic characters in the higher organisms. Among the investigators of cytologic and genetic phenomena (among the multicellulars) the belief is practically unanimous that the elaborate mechanism involved in nuclear division is primarily a design for distributing the factors concerned in heredity. Now it would be very strange indeed if a similar and quite as complicated a mechanism in ameba had no function to perform. For what would be the purpose of the complicated nuclear changes in ameba if not concerned with heredity? As has already been seen, however, there are numerous cytoplasmic characters, in the larger amebas at least, that are inherited from one generation to the next with as little variation as is observed in other organisms (Schaeffer, '16). The recent work of Jennings ('16) on *Difflugia* and Hegner ('18) on *Arcella* also indicates that the general processes of inheritance in these organisms which are closely related to amebas, are similar to those observed in higher forms. The conclusion seems justified therefore that the nuclear changes in amebas mean essentially the same thing as in other organisms.

We are now therefore in a position to say that amebas are definitely and thoroughly organized; that they are not really "shapeless"; that they are not more subject to variation than a higher organism is; and that each species differs from all others in probably every visible detail. The large variety of pseudopods observed in different species are seen not to be the result of physical or extrinsic chemical forces acting upon ectoplasms differing in some mere physical character as viscosity. But all these peculiarities are hereditary, and are due to a fundamental chemical structure of the protoplasm which is specific for the species. The highly characteristic nature of the pseudopods formed by the amebas of any species, it is seen, is to be referred to the fundamental structure of the protoplasm, probably its stereochemical structure. And what is of especial importance for this discussion, the character of streaming concerned with pseudopod formation and with movement in general, which is specific for each species, is likewise found, to some extent at least, to be conditioned by the specific structure of the protoplasm.

That the specific character of the pseudopods, and the streaming which of course lies back of it, is not wholly or perhaps even largely, due to the specific structure of the protoplasm, is evident from a consideration of streaming in some other organisms, without a study of which, streaming in amebas can be only imperfectly understood.

The formation of pseudopods is not necessary to streaming. Occasionally one sees internal currents unaccompanied by movement or ectoplasm formation in amebas approximating spherical shape, such as in *Amoeba blattae* (Rhumbler, '98) and rarely also in *proteus* or *dubia*. But especially well is such streaming seen in a contracted *Biomyxa*, a naked foraminifer, and in numerous plant cells. In paramecium and other ciliates the continuous circulation of the endoplasm,—a true streaming process,—is an involuntary act. But in *Frontonia*, another large ciliate, the circulation of the endoplasm is under the control of the animal, that is to say, voluntary, and is set in motion only when feeding, the direction of streaming being away from the mouth so as to drag in the food (see Figure 32, p. 99). If the food particle is a long filament of *Oscillatoria*, for example, the endoplasm circulates very much as it does in paramecium, only more rapidly, until the whole filament is wound up into a coil. Then streaming stops. In the second place streaming is not necessarily accompanied by the formation of ectoplasm as observed in ameba. In plant cells the ectoplasm is practically stationary, while the endoplasm is in continual flux. The transformation of endoplasm into ectoplasm and vice versa is therefore not an essential feature of streaming, though it is of locomotion; that is, ectoplasm is always found between endoplasm and water, though it might be possible under certain conditions for endoplasm to come into contact with water without stiffening. And if so, there appears to be no reason why locomotion might not occur. It appears however under normal conditions that a moderate tendency to ectoplasm formation (*proteus*, *dubia*) leads to greater efficiency in movement than a very weak (*limicola*) or a very strong (*verrucosa*) tendency to form ectoplasm.

In the reticulose rhizopods, as is well known there is no ectoplasm of the kind observed in amebas. The middle of the pseudopod, moreover, is not the region of most rapid streaming as in ameba, but frequently becomes congealed, on the contrary, into a rod-like structure. In general this axial rod has the character of very stiff ectoplasm. The character of streaming in reticulose rhizopods, however, has received very little attention, and detailed comparisons are therefore impossible.

Another interesting property of reticulose pseudopods, which are formed by a streaming process, is their great power in some species, of rapid contraction. If a diatom for example, in its movements breaks loose a pseudopod it is often (though not necessarily) contracted very rapidly, much more rapidly than could be the case if it were accomplished by streaming. It frequently happens that knobs are found on a slender pseudopod. These knobs may move back and forth with great rapidity without visibly affecting the pseudopod (Figure 12). The process reminds one of a block sliding on a rope. These observations indicate a very high degree of elasticity in the formed pseudopods of such a rhizopod as *Biomyxa* as compared with a very low degree of elasticity in the amebas.

It thus appears that the process of streaming is a much more fundamental phenomenon than most of the theories accounting for ameboid movement would lead one to suppose; for these theories concern themselves only with streaming as observed in amebas, and many content themselves with only two or three species. Since the general features of streaming are similar no matter where streaming occurs, no theory is likely to gain acceptance that explains streaming only in one group of organisms. Streaming in rhizopods, myxomycetes, ciliates, plant cells, is most rationally looked upon as caused by the same fundamental process; but the detailed form it takes, especially in freely formed pseudopods, is undoubtedly conditioned by the structure of the protoplasm, both physically and chemically, but more especially the latter.

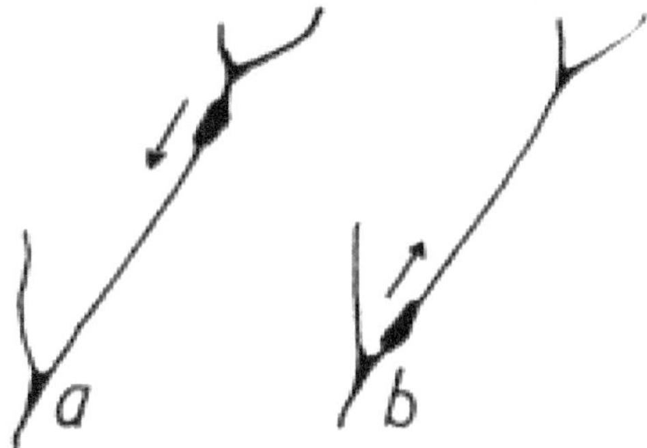

FIGURE 12

Illustrating the high degree of elasticity in the pseudopods of *Biomyxa vagans*. In *a* and *b* are shown two stages of a small section of the pseudopodial network, which remained unchanged while a small lump of protoplasm (near the arrow) moved rapidly up and down the slender pseudopod. Movement along the whole length of the pseudopod occupied about half a second. Just exactly what the movement was due to could not be determined, but the distance between the forks in the pseudopod did not change, nor did the thickness of the protoplasmic strand on which the protoplasmic lump moved change noticeably.

CHAPTER VII

EXPERIMENTS ON THE SURFACE LAYER OF THE AMEBA

In the preceding chapters we have discussed the streaming of the endoplasm in various representative species of ameba, and its transformation into ectoplasm at the anterior end. We have observed that the details of streaming are not quite the same for any two species of ameba, and that in consequence the character of locomotion also is specific for every ameba. All the observations prove that movement in ameba is always associated with streaming, and streaming (in locomotion) with ectoplasm formation. It follows therefore that the form of movement observed in amebas depends invariably upon the streaming of the endoplasm accompanied by the formation of ectoplasm.

There is however another element which, although it appears to be a consequence of ectoplasm formation, must nevertheless be included in any account of ameboid movement because of the light it is bound to shed on the physical processes concerned in streaming. This element is the thin outer layer which separates the water in which the ameba lives from the ectoplasm. It is the properties of this layer to which we may now direct our attention.

That such a layer exists was indicated by observations of Bütschli ('92) and Blochmann ('94), as already mentioned; but neither of these authors stated definitely whether they considered a third layer actually to exist or whether the ectoplasm as such moved forward. Jennings ('04), as has been pointed out, concluded that no third layer exists and that the particles clinging to the outsides of amebas, which are carried toward the anterior end, are carried by the ectoplasm. Gruber ('12) concluded however that an outer layer exists, composed of gelatinous substance, which moves ahead at about the same rate as the ectoplasm (p. 373). According to Gruber's view the outer layer is a permanently differentiated layer of material. Schaeffer ('17), on the contrary calls it a layer of protoplasm, which moves forward faster than the forward advance of the ameba.

It is a very simple matter to demonstrate the existence of this layer. Although any insoluble non-toxic substance of low specific gravity such as carmine or soot, when reduced to very small particles and mixed with the water in which the amebas to be examined live, will cling to the outside of the ameba so that the movement of the outer layer can be observed; in my experience the best as well as the most convenient substance to use is the dried flocculent colloidal sediment from ameba cultures, rubbed to powder with the ball of the finger. This powder swells up in water into flocculent masses which are large for their weight and do not show such active Brownian movement as particles of carmine or india ink, and they consequently adhere more easily to the ameba. Moreover no foreign substances are thereby introduced into the water.

FIGURE 13.

Amoeba sphaeronucleosus. In locomotion. Note the nucleus, contractile vacuole, ectoplasmic ridges. This ameba is not known to form pseudopods. Length, 120 microns.

Of the more common species of amebas, those with the firmer ectoplasms are the most favorable for studying the movements of the outer layer. We may therefore first take up several observations on *Amoeba sphaeronucleosus* (Figure 13). This ameba resembles the more common *A. verrucosa.* It is about 120 microns long and is usually of an oval shape in locomotion. It is more active and less disturbed by jars than *verrucosa.*

Figure 14 represents a *sphaeronucleosus* with a small particle attached to the middle of the upper surface of the ameba. As the ameba moves forward, shown by successive outlines, the particle likewise moves forward, but, as will be observed, at a more rapid rate. Measuring the distance from particle outline 1 to 4, and from ameba outline 1 to 4, it is seen that the rate of movement of the particle compares with the rate of movement of the ameba as 2.48 to 1.

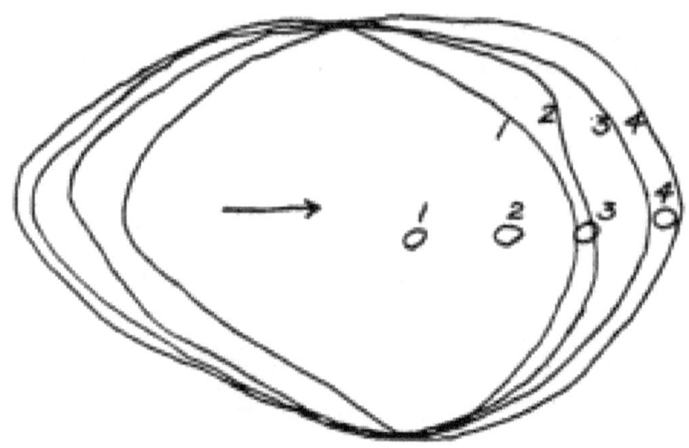

FIGURE 14.

Illustrating the movement of a particle on the upper surface layer
of an *Amoeba sphaeronucleosus*. Length of the ameba, 120 microns.

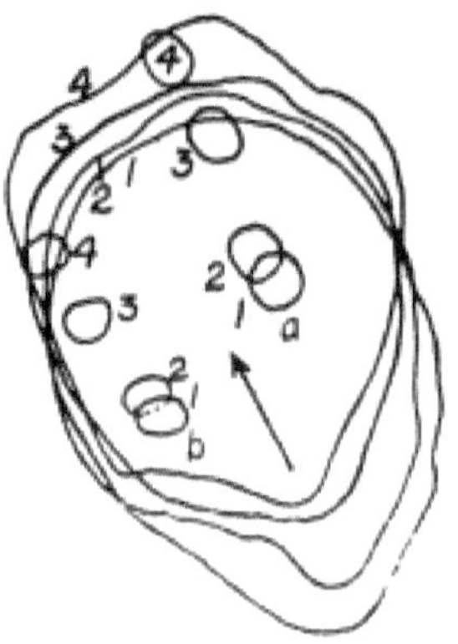

FIGURE 15.

An *Amoeba sphaeronucleosus* with two particles attached to its upper surface film, one in the middle and one at the side. *a* moved
2.6 times as fast as the ameba while *b*, lying nearer the side, moved
only 1.9 times as fast as the ameba. Length, 100 microns.

Particles lying near the side do not move forward as rapidly as those lying in
the middle. Figure 15 shows two particles, one of which, *a*, lying near the middle
of the ameba, moved 2.6 times as fast as the ameba advanced in the region of the
particle; while particle *b* moved only 1.9 as fast as the ameba in front of the particle.
The speed ratio of particle *a* to particle *b* was as 1.26 to 1.

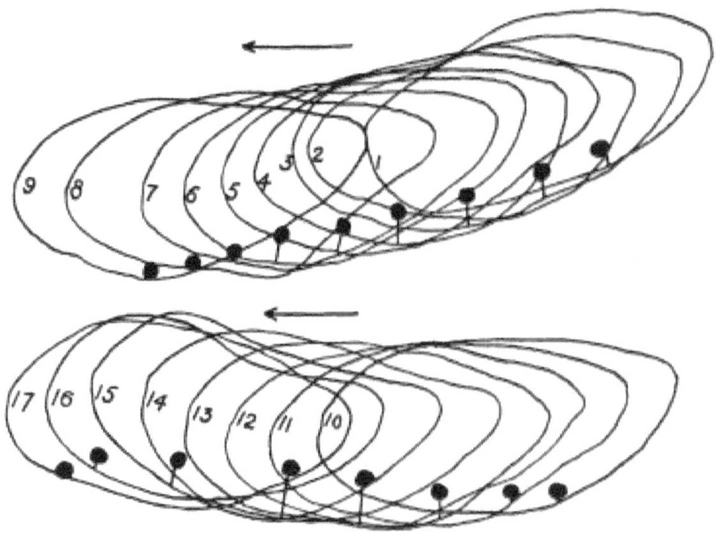

FIGURE 16.

Illustrating more rapid movement of the surface film in the middle of *Amoeba sphaeronucleosus* than near the edge. The vertical lines connecting the particle with the ameba outlines were drawn only for convenience of reference. Length of ameba, 120 microns.

Figure 16 shows a particle lying still more to the side than in the preceding figure. In the first six stages the particle moved 1.85 times as fast as the ameba. The particle then came to the edge. From stage 7 to 10 the particle moved more slowly than the ameba. At stage 11 the particle had come to lie in the posterior half of the ameba, where the tendency of the surface layer is to travel toward the middle of the upper surface. In stage 12 the particle had gotten away from the edge of the ameba and already shows a gain in speed. From stage 13 to 16 the particle moved again about 1.83 times as fast as the ameba. But at stage 16 the edge was reached with a consequent decrease in speed of the particle.

The direction of the path described by a particle carried on the back of an ameba depends upon what part of the ameba is most rapidly forming ectoplasm. That is, the particle tends to

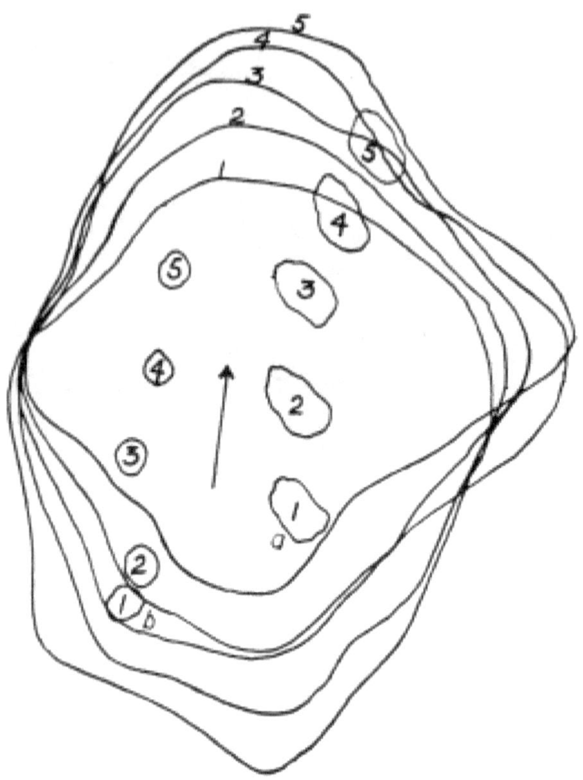

FIGURE 17.

Illustrating the different speeds with which particles move when attached to the surface film of an *Amoeba sphaeronucleosus*, depending upon their location. Particle *a* moved 3.5 times as fast as the ameba and *b* 2.7 times as fast. Length of ameba, 110 microns.

move toward that part of the anterior edge that is advancing most rapidly. Figures 17 and 18 illustrate this point. Figure 17 shows an ameba with two particles on its back, and with an unequally advancing anterior edge. Particle *a* moved more rapidly than *b* because: (1) it was moving away from a more rapidly receding posterior region; (2) the right anterior edge was advancing more rapidly than the left anterior edge; (3) the particle was nearer the anterior edge. The rapidly advancing right edge in stage 4 accounts for the veering of the particle *a* to the right. The more rapid advance of *b* from stage 3 to 5 is due to the remoteness of the anterior right edge, which, because of its nearness to particle a pulls on it to a much greater extent than on particle *b*. That is to say, when a particle lies somewhere *between* two rapidly growing regions on the anterior edge, leading in different directions, that particle is attracted to the edge less rapidly than a particle lying immediately back of either advancing region. As may readily be observed each change in speed or direction of movement of the particle *b* finds its explanation in the amount and location of ectoplasm formation at the time. Large particles like *a* do not so readily reflect changes in the direction of pull of the surface layer.

The rapid rate of movement of particle *a*—3.5 times as fast as the ameba— finds its explanation in an actively advancing anterior edge that was unusually wide. Particle *b* moved at a slower rate, 2.7 to 1. It started from near the posterior edge where it moved comparatively slowly for a short distance.

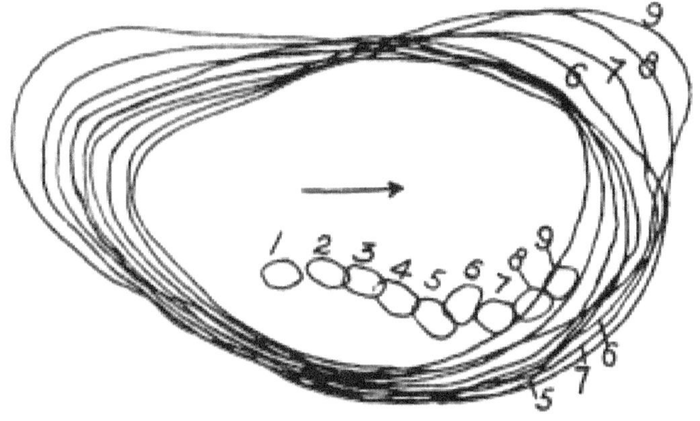

FIGURE 18.

Illustrating the effect on the path of a particle attached to the surface film of an *Amoeba sphaeronucleosus* when the ameba changes its direction of movement. From stages 3 to 5 the ameba veered to the right, also the particle. From stages 6 to 9 the ameba turned sharply to the left, and this change of direction was reflected in the movement of the particle. Length of the ameba, about 120 microns.

Figure 18 shows more pronounced changes in the direction taken by a particle attached to the back of an ameba. The change in direction at stage 6 was caused by a wave of ectoplasm thrown out at the left side, and cessation of movement at the anterior edge. At 7 a small wave was thrown out at the anterior edge and a large wave on the left. At stages 8 and 9 the direction of the particle was again a response to the waves of ectoplasm thrown out at the left anterior edge, which thus became the anterior end.

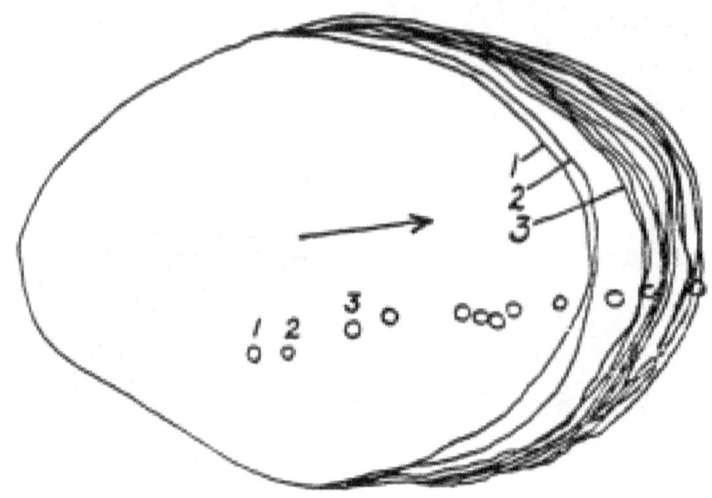

FIGURE 19.

Illustrating the rapid movement of the upper surface of an *Amoeba sphaeronucleosus* under the most favorable conditions. The particle moved 3.56 times as fast as the ameba. Length of the ameba, 130 microns.

The movement of particles on the under side of an *Amoeba sphaeronucleosus* depends upon what part of the ameba is attached to the substratum. Where the ameba is attached there is of course no movement of the surface layer and the particles remain stationary. In an ameba attached as shown in figure 20, *a*, there was a very slow movement of particles forward near the middle of the attached region (x), but whether this was related to the movement of the outer layer of the upper surface was not determined. The movement of these particles was considerably slower than the movement of the ameba. In another ameba attached at the anterior and posterior ends (Figure 20, *b*) no movement of particles on the under side could be discerned. The small particles showing Brownian movement, with the surrounding water, are dragged along as a mass. This movement is purely mechanical, and is what would be expected on purely physical grounds, when a more or less cup-shaped object is moved along in water in close contact with a flat surface. Such particles as have become attached to the surface layer on the under side of the ameba, because of their slower movement than that of the ameba, eventually bring up at the sides near the posterior end, as the ameba moves along. From here they are carried forward in the manner already described. Thus there comes about a "rotation" of particles adhering to an ameba as described by Jennings ('04) and Dellinger ('06), though the explanation is different from that given by Jennings (l. c.) as we shall see further on. No case of a similar rotation of larger particles which had sunk into the ectoplasm, as described by Jennings ('04, p. 142), has come under my observation.

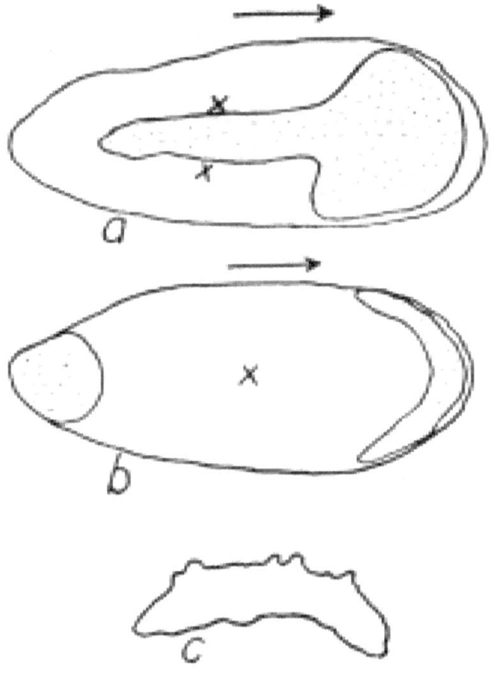

FIGURE 20.

Amoeba sphaeronucleosus. a, the under side of the ameba. The part of the ameba attached to the substratum is stippled. Particles attached to the surface film at *x* moved slowly forward. *b*, the under side of the ameba, showing the attached parts stippled. The particles suspended in the water at *x* moved slowly forward with the ameba. *c*, a cross section of an ameba of shape shown in *b*, showing the ridges on the surface. Length of the ameba, about 100 microns.

The movement of the surface layer in *A. verrucosa* is quite like that of *sphaeronucleosus*. Figure 21 shows a group of three particles carried by a *verrucosa* while changing its direction of locomotion. The particles changed position with regard to each other and they moved at different speeds. Particles *a, b, c*, moved respectively 2.40, 3.26, 2.85 times as fast as the ameba advanced. Other experiments indicate that the outer layer of *verrucosa* moves at about the same speed, compared with the speed of the ameba, as that of *sphaeronucleosus*.

Amebas with so-called limax-shaped bodies do not possess surface layers that carry particles forward with the same speed as those amebas with broad bodies. It is only occasionally that large amebas such as *proteus* are found in a limax or clavate shape. One of the most favorable of the large amebas in this respect is *discoides*. It is frequently found in clavate shape and it possesses the further advantage in being nearly cylindrical in cross section. It is also more in the habit of loping along the surface in the manner described by Dellinger ('06, p. 57) so that what is observed to take place in *discoides* in the clavate shape, holds likewise for free pseudopods extended into the water out of contact with a solid support (Figure 22).

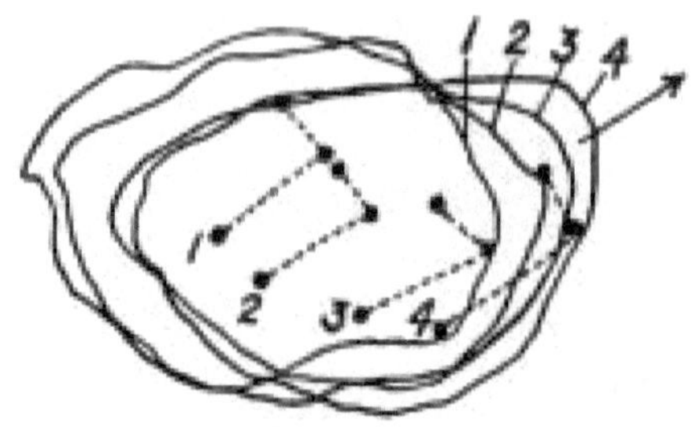

FIGURE 21.

Illustrating the similarity of the movement of the surface layer of *Amoeba verrucosa* with that of *A. sphaeronucleosus*. A group of three particles, connected by dotted lines for reference, change their relative positions as the ameba (*verrucosa*) changes its direction of movement. Length of the ameba, 150 microns.

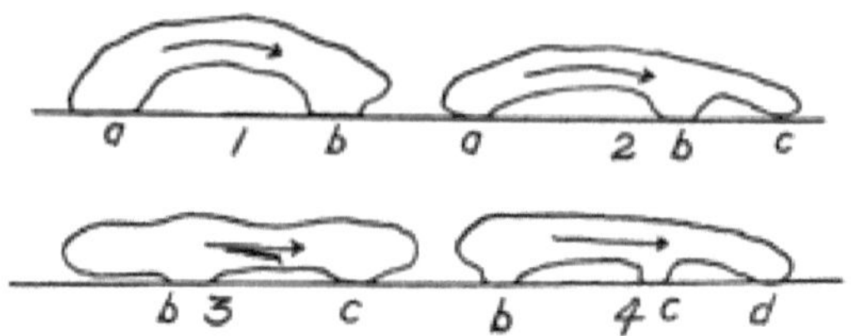

FIGURE 22.

Illustrating the movements of an *Amoeba proteus*, after Dellinger. At *c* in stage 2 a pseudopod is projected which fastens itself to the substratum as shown at *c*, 3, while *a*, 2, is pulled loose. In 4 another pseudopod is projected which fastens itself at *d*. The ameba is not in contact with the substratum at all points on its under side.

In figure 23 is shown a clavate *discoides* with a small particle attached to its side. The particle moved forward until it came to lie at the anterior edge, 10. The speed of the particle from 1 to 10 was 1.36 times as fast as that of the ameba, a much slower rate than was observed in *sphaeronucleosus*. At 6 a new pseudopod was projected for a short distance, thus increasing the amount of new ectoplasm forming in proportion to that of the whole ameba. This change was reflected in the increased speed of the particle, which moved 1.64 times as fast as the ameba from 5 to 6. At 10 the anterior end again spread out and again the particle moved faster — twice as fast as the ameba from 9 to 10. Stages 11, 12, 13 are added to show that the particles do not tend to go to the under surface but remain at or very near the tip.

The slight irregularity of the waves of hyaloplasm pushed out at the anterior end accounts for the changing position of the particle after it has reached the anterior edge. The particle remained at the edge of the advancing ameba for several minutes after the stage drawn at 13.

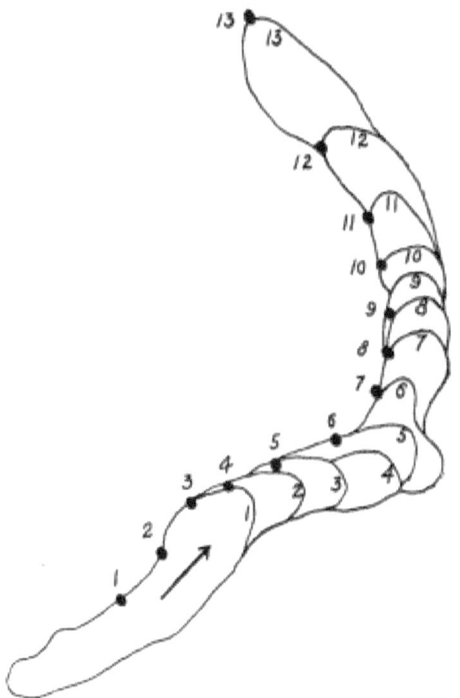

FIGURE 23.

Showing the movement of a particle on the surface layer of an *Amoeba discoides*. The particle remained on the anterior end of the ameba for several minutes after stage 13. The ameba was about 320 microns long.

In another observation the effect of a narrowing of the advancing tip of the ameba is shown very well. In figure 24 the ameba was advancing with a broad anterior end, as shown at 1 and 2. From 2 to 4, the region where new ectoplasm was made, narrowed down very considerably. These changes in the width of the anterior end are reflected, as in Figure 17 by a decrease in the relative speed of the moving particle. Thus the particle moved 1.75 times as fast as the ameba from 1 to 2 while from 2 to 4 the particle moved only 1.27 times as fast as the ameba.

FIGURE 24.

Showing the effect of a narrow anterior end on the rate of movement of the surface. Length of the ameba, about 320 microns.

The movement of the third layer in *proteus* is difficult to study owing to the formation continually of ridges, as explained on page 20. Even in clavate shaped amebas, waves of protoplasm are pushed out on the sides and on the tip with consequent formation of ectoplasm, so that the ameba grows in width slowly at the same time that it grows in length. A typical shape of a *proteus* in clavate form is slightly tapering toward the anterior end. This shape is maintained by gradual extension of the sides of the anterior half or two-thirds of the ameba as it moves along. These conditions are just the reverse of what was seen to be the case in *sphaeronucleosus* and *verrucosa*, where the anterior edge was wider than any other part of the body. But *discoides*, although free from the ridges and grooves characteristic of *proteus*, frequently has an anterior edge that is narrower than any part of the body, thus necessitating extension of the sides as the ameba moves forward.

Let us now see what is the effect of ridge formation upon the movement of the surface layer. Figure 25 shows a *proteus* and a narrow anterior end in *proteus* with two pseudopods and a particle attached to the side of the ameba at 1. Both pseudopods advanced until stage 4 was reached, but the particle was not appreciably deflected from an approximately straight path by the small pseudopod at the other side of the ameba. Reference to the figure shows that the particle travelled much faster while the pseudopod on the side was extending than after it began to retract. The particle moved 1.43 times as fast as the ameba from 1 to 4. But from 4 to 7 the particle moved only 1.06 times as fast as the ameba.

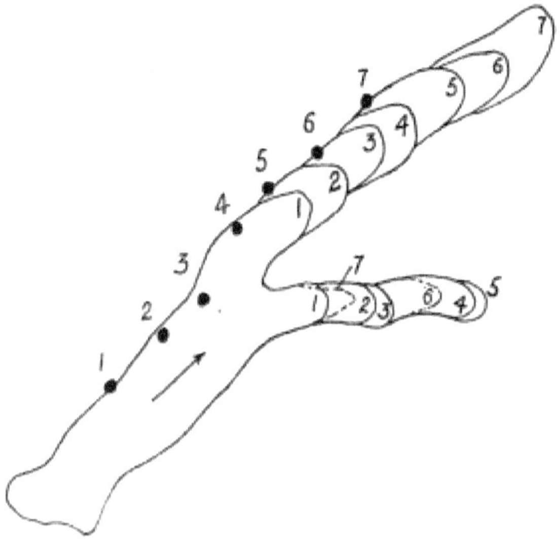

FIGURE 25.

Amoeba proteus. Rate of movement of the surface layer as compared with the rate of movement of the ameba. The pseudopod on the right was extended to stage 5; from then on it was retracted, as indicated by the outlines. Length of the ameba, 400 microns.

In the earlier stages the outer layer was pulled toward the tip of both pseudopods, in the later stages only toward one, and in this lies the explanation for a more rapid movement of the particles in the earlier, and a slower movement in the later stages. This effect was also observed in *discoides*, but the fact that the particle in the later stages moved only very little faster than the ameba is due to a narrow anterior edge and to the formation of ectoplasm in the ridges over the surface of the ameba. The effect of ridge formation on the movement of particles attached to the surface film is well seen when an ameba has two forward moving regions opposite each other. Under such conditions particles located equidistant or nearly so between such regions, move only very slowly or not at all, the pull upon the film being nearly or quite equal. In a similar manner the ridges which are constantly forming on a *proteus* are continually competing with the anterior end in their pull upon the surface layer, thus preventing rapid forward movement.

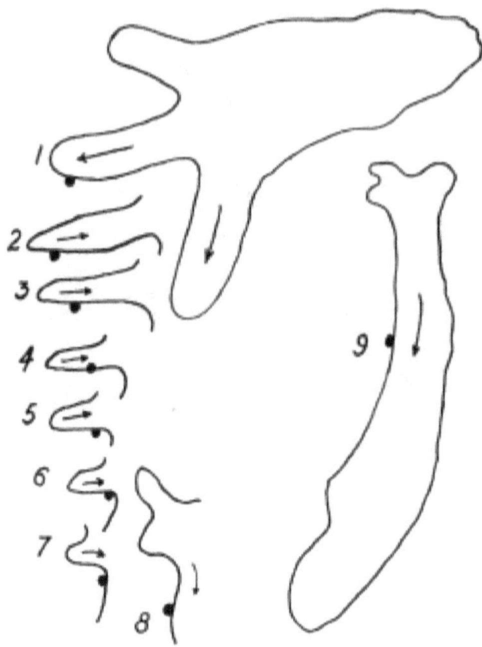

FIGURE 26.

Showing the comparative rate of movement of the surface film
over the retracting parts of the ameba. In figures 2 to 8 only a part
of the ameba is shown. Length of the ameba, 500 microns.

Figure 26 shows that the surface layer flows away from the tip of a retracting pseudopod that is located near the anterior end. The particle moves slowly until the body of the ameba is reached, when movement becomes more rapid, 8, 9. This proves that the third layer moves away from the retracting parts of an ameba, no matter how large the total area of these parts may be in proportion to the area of new surface that is being made. But whether the speed of the moving third layer changes in correspondence with a larger or a smaller ratio between building and retracting ectoplasm has not been ascertained.

Figure 27 shows that the relative positions of particles attached to the surface layer may readily change while the ameba deploys its psuedopods.

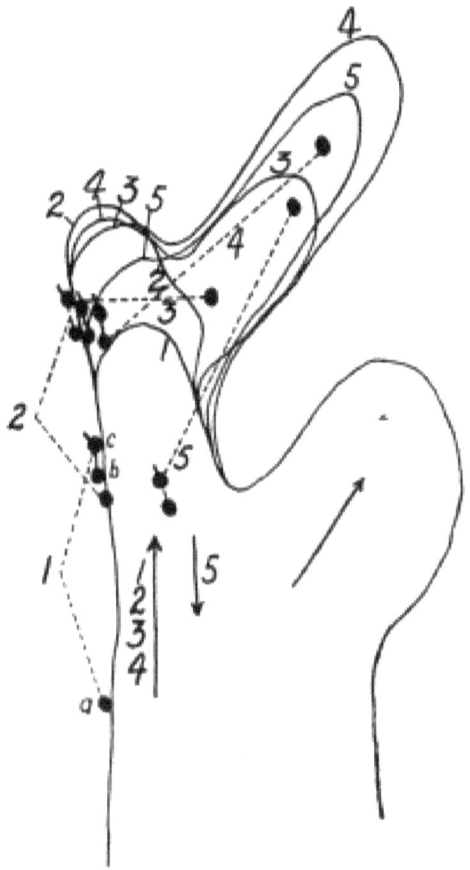

FIGURE 27.

A part of an *Amoeba proteus* illustrating what is perhaps the most characteristic quality of the surface layer of amebas, its fluid nature. Three particles, *a, b, c,* were moving forward along an actively growing pseudopod. In stage 2, particles *b* and *c* had arrived nearly at the tip of the pseudopod. A pseudopod was then thrown out on the right, which resulted in the movement of *a* in the same direction, while *b* and *c* remained nearly stationary. Later on this pseudopod was retracted. *b* and *c* were drawn back toward the main body of the ameba while *c* remained behind, moving only very slowly. Thus the relative positions of these particles was completely changed.

Three particles marked *a, b, c* and connected by a line for convenience of reference, were in the position indicated at 1 when the forward end of the ameba occupied the position indicated by outline 1. As the ameba moved forward the particle *c* gained slightly on *a* and *b* for no ascertainable reason, unless it was on account of the projection of the large pseudopod on the opposite side. At stage 2 a new pseudopod was started on the right, which at stage 3 had grown to large size while streaming in the original pseudopod was arrested. At stage 3 particles a and b retained the same position they had in stage 2, except for a slight turning to the right. Particle c however moved across the base of the original pseudopod and on to the middle of the new pseudopod. At stage 4 a and b had again only slightly moved to the right of the position they occupied in stages 2 and 3, while c moved rapidly toward the tip of the new pseudopod. The new pseudopod was then retracted and at stage 5 the particles had begun to move back toward the main body of the ameba. Particles a and b now gained considerably on c because they were located further away from the tip of the retracting pseudopod. Particles a and b were drawn to the middle of the retracting pseudopod because of the continuous enlargement of the large pseudopod on the right, below, through which the ameba moved on.

The most important feature of this observation is the change in the position of the particle c with respect to that of a and b. The latter particles retained their relative positions with very slight, if any, change, while c swung around a and b nearly $180°$, and at the same time changed the distance very greatly between itself and the other particles. Moreover, b, at stage 5 led the procession of particles, while at stage 1, a led. No further demonstration is necessary to show that the surface layer is distinctly fluid and dynamic, and not at all such a static structure as an elastic permanent skin, as Jennings ('04) and Rhumbler ('14) maintained.

CHAPTER VIII
ON THE NATURE OF THE SURFACE LAYER

The observations in the preceding chapters on the general movements of the surface layer of amebas will afford a sufficient basis for an inquiry into the nature of this layer. The mere demonstration of the existence of this layer is, of course, interesting enough, for a number of contradictory statements by various students of the amebas are satisfactorily cleared up by these observations. But the problem of ameboid movement affects other organisms besides amebas, and since the movement of the surface layer is so intimately associated with ameboid movement, it becomes of more than ordinary interest to learn something of the nature and composition of this layer.

In the first place the property of carrying particles toward the anterior end of amebas does not appear to be of any advantage. That is, whatever the movements of the outer layer may be, the ameba does not appear to be better off when particles are carried forward than when none are carried, for such particles are very small and almost without exception devoid of food value. The particles are masses of debris which accidentally adhere to the ameba, and the ameba makes no visible effort to make such particles adhere, nor to get rid of them. The ameba seems to be quite indifferent to the presence of such particles.

On the other hand, as Schaeffer ('17) has pointed out, the capacity for transporting particles cannot but be looked upon as a hindrance to locomotion. As has been stated, the surface film moves in the same direction as the ameba. Whenever the surface film comes against a solid object, it pushes against the object, and nullifies to a certain, though small, extent the energy expended in moving forward. And it will be seen without further argument, of course, that the energy involved in carrying particles forward is not only itself lost but consumes an appreciable part of the energy available for forward movement. This fact, together with the universal occurrence of this phenomenon among amebas indicates beyond question that it is intimately associated with ameboid movement as it is ordinarily understood in amebas, and that it is almost certainly a "necessary" physical consequence of the more fundamental physical processes involved in the movement of amebas.

That the third layer moves in the same general direction as the ameba has already been mentioned. The direction of a moving particle is however not necessarily parallel with the stream of endoplasm below. In a retracting pseudopod that lies nearly parallel to and by the side of the main advancing pseudopod, the particles on the far side and near the base frequently move across the pseudopod at an angle (and therefore also across the endoplasmic stream), and up the active pseudopod on the near side. This shows conclusively that the direction of flowing endoplasm by itself has no direct connection with the direction of flow of the surface layer.

To say that the particles carried by the surface layer bring up at the anterior ends of pseudopods or of the ameba when in clavate shape, admits of further qualification. The advancing edge is not a straight line but an arc, and the sides near the advancing edge are building at a slower rate than the extreme tip. The most rapid formation of ectoplasm is at that point of the ameba that is farthest ahead. At this point all the ectoplasm to be made is still to be made, but as one passes back along the side of the pseudopod more and more ectoplasm is encountered and less and less remains to be made. There is therefore a gradient in the rate and in the amount of ectoplasm formed as one passes back from the forward end of the longitudinal axis of the pseudopod along the side. This is especially the case with certain amebas like *Amoeba discoides, A. laureata* and others in which the pseudopods are more nearly cylindrical. In such amebas as *A. proteus* and *A. verrucosa*, the factor of ridge formation complicates to some extent the longitudinal gradient of ectoplasm formation. But in spite of these specific differences, the general statement still holds that the rate of ectoplasm formation at the extreme anterior end is higher than anywhere else in the ameba, and that the rate gradually falls to zero as the nearly straight and parallel sides of the pseudopod or ameba, as the case may be, are approached.

Now we have seen that if a particle becomes attached to the outer layer of such an ameba as discoides, which has nearly symmetrical pseudopods, at some considerable distance from the tip of the pseudopod, it moves forward until the tip of the pseudopod is reached. It does not tend to come to rest near the tip of the pseudopod, where the rate of ectoplasm formation is much higher than at the sides of the pseudopod, though not as high as at the tip, but it moves on until the tip is reached. That is, the movement of particles on the surface film is toward that small area at the extreme anterior end where the rate of ectoplasm formation is highest.

In such an ameba as *verrucosa*, however, the highest rate of ectoplasm formation would be, not at a small circular area, but a very narrow strip along the anterior edge; for the rate of ectoplasm formation over a considerable portion of the width of the anterior end of the ameba is practically the same, according to observation. Consequently we do not find particles which are attached to the outer layer tending to move to a point lying on the longitudinal axis, but their paths are found to be straight and parallel with the longitudinal axis, if headed toward any point over a considerable stretch of the anterior edge on either side of the longitudinal axis.

All the evidence that is at hand therefore points to the conclusion that the direction of movement of the surface film in a moving ameba is toward that point where ectoplasm is formed most rapidly.

But where do the particles come from? At exactly what regions of the ameba do they start to travel toward the anterior ends of the ameba? In *sphaeronucleosus* and its congeners, it is very difficult to determine just when the particles begin to move toward the forward edge. Particles near the posterior end on the upper surface of these amebas moved forward slowly, much more slowly than particles near the middle. Sometimes particles near the posterior end seem to be motionless for some time, but the incessant though slow kneading process going on at the posterior end makes accurate observation difficult. Only in a general way it may be stated that particles begin their forward march at or near the posterior end. In amebas that habitually form pseudopods more accurate information can be obtained.

In *proteus* or *discoides*, for example, projecting pseudopods are often suddenly stopped and retracted, with a resultant change of an anterior to a posterior end. Particles attached to the outer surface on such pseudopods move toward the anterior end, of course, as long as the pseudopod is building, in the manner described in the preceding pages. But when the endoplasmic stream is arrested, the forward movement of the particle likewise stops. When the endoplasm starts to flow back into the main body of the ameba, the particle also starts moving back; but there is a period of a few seconds after the endoplasmic stream is reversed during which the particle remains quiet. And when it does start in to move, it moves only slowly. Within a few seconds, however, the average speed of movement is attained. This is true of particles located some distance away from the tip of the pseudopod. If the particle has reached the tip of the pseudopod before reversal of the endoplasmic stream takes place, the particle often remains at the tip until the pseudopod is almost completely withdrawn into the main body of the ameba (Figure 26, p. 60). At other times such a particle becomes displaced, presumably by irregular retraction of the tip of the pseudopod, and finds itself at the side of the pseudopod. When this happens it moves slowly toward the main body of the ameba, but faster than the tip of the pseudopod does.

It frequently happens, especially in *annulata*, but also in *proteus* and other forms with many pseudopods, that when an advancing pseudopod is about to be withdrawn, there intervenes a stage where the endoplasm in the distal part moves away from the ameba, while that in the proximal part moves toward the ameba, with a neutral or motionless zone between. In such case a particle on the distal end moves slowly toward the tip while a particle in the proximal region moves toward the base of the pseudopod. Particles over the neutral zone are motionless. In these cases, however, changes in the direction and speed of the ectoplasmic stream are too frequent and the relative strengths of the distal and proximal currents too variable, to enable one to secure very accurate data by means of camera lucida drawings (a kinematograph is essential for this purpose), so no figures of the speed of movement of such particles are given. Nevertheless the general results of the observations are as stated. It might be added that in some cases the neutral zone for the particles attached to the surface did not coincide exactly with the neutral zone of the endoplasm, but was located a little further distally.

From these observations it appears that a rough index of the direction of movement of the surface film is the direction of the streaming of the endoplasm; and that the surface layer moves away from regions where ectoplasm is in the process of being converted into endoplasm. Since a particle attached to the surface may remain for some time at the tip of a retracting pseudopod, while one that is attached to the sides of a pseudopod moves toward its base, it appears that the speed of the moving surface film is not directly correlated to the rate of transformation of ectoplasm into endoplasm. The slower speed of particles near the posterior end points also in this direction. The formation of ectoplasm at the anterior end seems therefore to be much more intimately connected with the movement of the surface film than the destruction of the ectoplasm, though it is not yet clear that the liquefaction of the ectoplasm is altogether without effect.

Now as to the speed with which the surface film moves. The foregoing illustrations and figures show that the particles attached to a *sphaeronucleosus* on the upper surface move from 2.5 to 3.6 times as fast as the ameba (Figure 19) while particles attached to a *discoides* move only from 1.2 to 2 times as fast as the ameba moves. In *proteus* the speed of the particles is still slower, because of the longitudinal ridge-like waves of protoplasm which are continually being thrown out. In this species it frequently happens that because of the numerous ridges, the ameba moves faster than the particles attached to the outer surface; but this is to be looked upon as a mechanical complication, not as indicating a difference in the nature of the surface layer.

How is the difference in the speed of movement of the surface layer between *sphaeronucleosus* and *discoides* to be explained? There are no ridges to retard the movement of particles in *discoides*, while there are ridges in *sphaeronucleosus*, where the particles move on the average twice as fast as on *discoides*. In the first place the advancing edge, the edge where ectoplasm is being made, is proportionately much wider in *sphaeronucleosus* than in *discoides* as compared with the amount of surface back of it. Figures 23 and 24 show that the rate of movement of the surface film is directly proportional to the amount of new ectoplasm forming. In the second place, the greater part of the under surface in the forward half of *sphaeronucleosus* is attached to the substrate, so that the surface layer which flows toward the anterior end is derived almost wholly from the upper surface; while in *discoides* the whole surface in free pseudopods, and nearly the whole surface in attached amebas (cf. Dellinger's observations described on p. 56) possesses mobile surface protoplasm. Observation of moving particles on these amebas proves this. Then again, the anterior edge of a *sphaeronucleosus* is not attached at the points farthest advanced, but the point of attachment is some distance back, as indicated in figure 20. The effect of this is to increase the amount of forming ectoplasm in proportion to the surface of the ameba from which surface protoplasm may be drawn. Still one other factor must be considered. As is well known *sphaeronucleosus, verrucosa* and their congeners possess longitudinal ridges on the upper surface which consist of ectoplasm, covered of course by the surface film. These ridges are formed near the anterior edge, not by wrinkling, but by the construction of new ectoplasm. Once formed, they remain until the ameba, so to speak, flows out from under them. That is, the ridges undergo comparatively slight changes until changed back into endoplasm at the posterior end of the ameba. As the ameba flows ahead the ridges are of course continually being added to or lengthened, by the conversion of some endoplasm into ectoplasm. The ridges may thus retain their identity for a long time although the substance composing them is changed every time the ameba moves the length of its body. It is clear, therefore, that there is more ectoplasm formed at the anterior end of a *sphaeronucleosus* than would be the case were the upper surface of the ameba plane; and the conclusion therefore is obvious that the formation of ridges, occurring as it does, chiefly at the anterior end, serves further to accelerate the forward movement of the surface film.

If the form of *sphaeronucleosus* were more regular than it is, the amount of ectoplasm in the process of forming at any given moment could be compared with a similar relation existing in *discoides*, to see whether these respective ratios were proportional to the speed of the moving surface films in the two amebas. As it is, the irregularity of form of *sphaeronucleosus* makes such computation subject to the possibility of considerable error. In *discoides* however the problem is comparatively simple. I therefore did not go into this matter extensively, but merely worked out the relations mentioned in one case, and I mention it here to illustrate the method rather than to record the result, which is not to be taken as very exact.

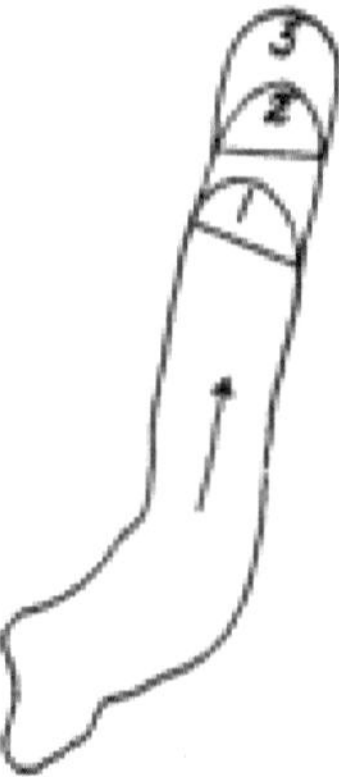

FIGURE 28.

A clavate *Amoeba discoides*, showing the amount of ectoplasm that
is constantly being made at the anterior end. Length of the ameba,
310 microns.

Since the movement of the surface film is obviously a surface phenomenon, only the surfaces of the amebas need to be taken into account. In Figure 28 is illustrated a *discoides* of such a shape as to allow a fairly accurate computation of its surface. Three outlines of the anterior end only are given; the rear portion of the ameba remained approximately the same size and shape in the three outlines. The cross lines at the anterior end divide the forming ectoplasm of the ameba from the formed. As will be noticed the cross lines are drawn through the intersections of two successive outlines. Computing the areas on both sides of the cross lines for the two outlines and averaging them, there is found a ratio of 1 to 10; one-eleventh of the total surface represents forming ectoplasm, and ten-elevenths formed ectoplasm. (One-twenty-second of the total surface was deducted for surface attached to the substratum.) *Sphaeronucleosus* stands in contrast with *discoides* for it is attached to the substratum over a much greater area and in consequence only a slight amount of surface is drawn from the under side. This ameba may therefore be regarded in this connection as of only one surface, the upper. That part of outline 1 in Figure 14 cut by outline 2 indicates, as in *discoides*, the region of forming ectoplasm, and the space between outlines 1 and 2 may be used as a basis of computation. New ectoplasm is formed in this zone and far enough back to include the tips of the longitudinal ridges, of which we have already spoken (Figure 13). The zone of forming ectoplasm would therefore be about twice as wide as the average width of the three zones between the successive outlines in the figure, and of approximately the same shape. On this basis, the surface occupied by forming ectoplasm is $^1/_{5.8}$ of the total surface, and the ratio of formed to forming ectoplasm is 4.8 to 1.

(For the sake of completeness, a few factors whose values cannot easily be computed may be mentioned. 1. The anterior edge is not attached to the substratum at its farthest point, but at some little distance back of the edge, thus increasing the relative amount or forming ectoplasm; but this is offset by the surface of a part of the under side at the posterior end where the surface layer is active. 2. The ectoplasm composing the ridges, which must be added to the formed ectoplasm, would increase the ratio, though only slightly).

Approximately twice as much ectoplasm is therefore in the process of formation in *sphaeronucleosus* as in *discoides* when compared with the formed ectoplasm in the respective amebas, over which the surface film is active. This ratio corresponds very well with the rate of movement of the outer surface in these amebas, which as we have seen is about twice as fast in *sphaeronucleosus* as in *discoides*.

Where does the surface layer come from and what becomes of it after it arrives at the anterior end? It moves continually forward as long as the ameba moves forward. There would seem to be a tendency therefore for it to accumulate at the end of a free pseudopod in such a form as *discoides*, and even under ordinary conditions of locomotion where there is occasional attachment to the substratum by very short pseudopods, the surface layer is continually moving toward the anterior end on practically all sides. Every time, therefore, that the ameba moves a little less than its own length, there would accumulate at the tip of the ameba, if it were not removed, an amount of surface layer equivalent to that which covers the whole ameba. No such accumulation can be detected however, from which we infer that it is removed as fast as brought there. And the posterior region of the ameba, which is the main source of the surface film, does not become poorer in this material by reason of its continual flow forward, but new surface is made continually to take the place of that moving forward. This process of destruction and creation of surface is accordingly rapid during active locomotion;—a *discoides*, moving approximately once its length at room temperature in two minutes, destroying therefore the equivalent of its entire coat of surface in that time; while a *sphaeronucleosus*, moving once its length in two or three minutes, destroys all its surface every minute.

From what has been said thus far, it must be apparent that there is striking resemblance between the general movement of the surface layer of the ameba, and of a surface tension layer in a drop of fluid in which the tension is changed at some point. Let us now inquire briefly into this resemblance.

As is well known the surface of a liquid in contact with another liquid, solid or gas, with which it does not mix, behaves like a stretched membrane, so that when the tension is reduced at any point the surface layer moves away from that point. A good illustration of the effect of a decrease of surface tension is found in a drop of clove or other oil with which some substance that reduces the surface tension, such as alcohol or soap, is brought into contact at one side. If previously some dust particles have been placed on the surface of the oil drop, it will be easy to see that the surface of the oil moves to the opposite side from where the alcohol or soap solution touched the oil. In practice it is a very simple matter to lower the surface tension of a drop of fluid as described, so as to show the movement of particles on the surface. Almost any liquid may be used for this purpose. But it is comparatively very difficult to *increase* the surface tension at some point of a drop of fluid in such a way as to cause particles on the surface to move toward that point. The principle underlying the movement of the surface film in both cases is however exactly the same; so, although it would be more desirable to compare the surface movements in a drop of fluid in which the surface tension is increased at some point, because this is what happens in an ameba during locomotion, we shall nevertheless find it necessary to consider a drop of fluid in which the surface tension has been lowered. The application of the illustration is readily made.

When the surface tension of a drop of fluid is lowered by bringing into contact with it some other substance that possesses this power, the surface rushes away at great speed in all directions from the point where the tension is lowered, because usually the tension is reduced very considerably. In this surface movement it is found that new surface is made where the tension is lowered and old surface is destroyed, that is, pulled into the interior over a large part of the surface opposite to where the tension is lowered. The speed of the surface movement is most rapid near the point where the tension is lowered and becomes gradually slower as the opposite side of the drop is approached, where there is no movement. This variation in speed of the moving surface seems to be due largely to the small area in which the tension is lowered as compared with the whole surface of the drop.

In the ameba the conditions are reversed. The surface layer moves *toward* a point with increasing speed, instead of away from a point. In both the ameba and the drop the greatest speed is attained near the small area where the change in surface tension occurs.

The behavior of large and heavy particles on the surface of a drop of fluid and on an ameba are similar. A heavy particle as of sand, or a small glass rod, laid on the ameba, is not moved by the surface layer. It forms an island of surface matter around which the moving surface layer flows. Precisely the same thing happens in surface layer movements in inanimate fluids.

Again in point of thinness there is no disagreement so far as microscopic observation goes. Neither the surface film on an ameba nor the surface film on a fluid can be directly observed microscopically to be different from the fluid below it. The surface layer is, as is generally believed, of molecular dimensions, and its thickness is beyond the limits of vision. Unless some special means is discovered therefore for making visible the surface film, such as a process of staining, it may be impossible to ascertain its ultimate structure directly, for it overlies a mass of heterogeneous fluid whose composition is constantly changing.

It seems to follow from what is observed of the surface tension layers of the fluids of physics that such layers must be of the same constitution as the body of the fluid over which the layer is formed, although, as is well known, the proportion of the ingredients in the surface layer is different from that in the body of the fluid. Now since the resemblance between the surface layer of an ameba and a surface layer on a drop of fluid has thus far been found to be complete, it is pertinent at this point to discuss Gruber's ('12) suggestion that the movement of particles forward on an ameba is due to the forward movement of an inert layer of mucus or gelatinous material secreted by the ameba.

To begin with, observation does not support Gruber's suggestion. No such layer can be seen. Such a layer, since it is shown to persist for several minutes at least, should remain after an ameba bursts, under experimental conditions, but no such remains can be seen. Its existence should be demonstrable by the use of dyes, but the evidence is negative. Indeed there is not any direct evidence that can be brought in support of the suggestion that this surface layer is gelatinous in composition. Moreover, as we have seen, the layer on the ameba that carries particles forward seems to be destroyed at the anterior end, for in what other way would particles remain at the anterior end after being brought there? But the supposition that a gelatinous layer might be drawn into the interior at the anterior end is also negatived by observation, for no very small particles clinging to or imbedded in the surface substance are ever drawn into the ameba, as would almost certainly be the case if the substance composing the layer were gelatinous. And as to supposing that this layer, if gelatinous, might behave essentially as a surface tension layer and therefore be drawn in at the anterior end of the ameba, this is contrary to the experience of physics; for the physical nature of the ameba would make it impossible for the ameba to have a surface layer of gelatinous matter. There do not seem to exist any grounds therefore for supposing that the outermost layer of an ameba, the layer that carries particles as described in the preceding pages, can consist of an inert substance as Gruber suggests.[4]

From these considerations, then it appears that all the evidence available, both direct and indirect, points to the conclusion that the behavior of the surface layer on the ameba resembles in general and in detail the behavior of a surface tension layer in an inert drop of fluid, and that we must regard the surface layer on the

[4] It is possible that Gruber was led to suggest a gelatinous composition for the layer in question on the strength of assertions made by several writers that amebas secrete mucus. It is true that amebas may be displaced by threads of mucus hanging to glass needles which has collected on the needles while manipulating the amebas in the culture medium, but that is not to be taken as evidence that the mucus is secreted by the amebas. Ameba cultures are always full of gelatinous material formed by bacteria. I have not thus far been able to convince myself that amebas actually secrete mucus.

ameba as a true surface tension layer. This layer is therefore a dynamic layer, containing free energy, and capable of performing work. It is physiologically distinct from ectoplasm, as ectoplasm is distinct physiologically from endoplasm. But the distinctive properties which the surface layer possesses are functions of its position. These properties clearly indicate that its constitution is protoplasmic, corresponding to the fluid parts of the internal protoplasm.

The surface layer of the ameba is probably identical with what is commonly called the *plasma membrane* or semi-permeable membrane as postulated by Overton ('07). The peculiar structure supposed to be possessed by plasma membranes are held to be due chiefly to surface forces. The fact that the surface layer of the ameba is continually being destroyed and re-created during locomotion does not support the view that the plasma membrane is of inert composition, as for example, lipoidal, as has been suggested. The observations, on the contrary, confirm Höber's ('11) view that the plasma membranes generally are living structures. But it may be regarded as certain that if lipoids are present in the protoplasm of the ameba, these substances, according to the principle of Willard Gibbs, will be found in higher concentration in the surface film than in the body of the ameba.

Perhaps the most important question that arises in connection with the surface layer of the ameba is: What causes it to move in the manner described? But we can do little more than ask the question. It has been seen that the surface film moves toward an area of increased tension rather than from an area where the tension has been lowered. However, since we are completely in the dark respecting the composition of the surface layer or of the fluid parts of the ameba, it is exceedingly hazardous to venture an explanation. If the surface layer should have its tension lowered by a concentration of lipoids in it, we would be faced by the necessity of explaining their removal at the anterior end. If we turn to electrical causes we meet again with great difficulties. An ameba moves with the electric current, when a current is passed through the water. The surface layer under these conditions behaves normally, as may be inferred from Jennings' ('04) figure on page 198. That is, the current controls the direction of the movement of the ameba, with the current leaving the ameba at the point of highest surface tension. This is contrary to the action of the mercuric capillary electrometer, in which the mercury column also moves with the current, but because of lowered surface tension where the current leaves the mercury. The conditions surrounding these cases are so different however, that very little can be gained by setting them in contrast to each other.

CHAPTER IX

THE SURFACE LAYER AND THEORIES OF AMEBOID MOVEMENT

The observations recorded in the preceding two chapters, while they do not tell us anything about the direct cause of the movement of the surface layer, nevertheless indicate clearly enough that the area where ectoplasm is made is the area toward which the surface film flows. There is no question therefore of the intimate relation between the transformation of endoplasm into ectoplasm and the movement of the surface layer.

The apparent absence of movement in the surface film of the pseudopods of *Difflugia* (Schaeffer, '17) and the definitely proved absence of movement in the surface layer in the foraminiferan *Biomyxa* and myxomycete plasmodia, where no ectoplasm is formed in the manner observed in amebas, also indicates a causal relation between movement of the surface layer and ectoplasm formation. The relation moreover seems to be a necessary one for the movement of the surface layer is contrary to the processes involved in locomotion. In other words, from the standpoint of the ameba, it is a "necessary evil," so far as locomotion is concerned.

The transformation of endoplasm into ectoplasm is unfortunately not understood, though from what we know in a general way of the behavior of colloidal solutions it seems to be a surface tension effect due to (or accompanying) a change of phase. Something akin to gelation occurs as Kite ('13) has shown. It is a problem in the chemistry of colloids. But the structure or composition of the protoplasm is complex and practically unknown, and it is quite open to criticism whether analogies from the behavior of pure solutions of colloids, such as gelatin, afford any real basis for an explanation.

Although a knowledge of the movements of the surface layer is interesting enough by itself, it will achieve its true importance only when it can be related to other processes in the ameba in a causal manner. It does not at present give us any greater insight into the ultimate cause of ameboid movement, although it is clear that an important step in this direction has been taken. But no theory of ameboid movement can be accepted that demands conditions in the ameba that are contrary to those described in the preceding chapters, in connection with the surface layer. From this point of view therefore the discovery of the true nature of the outside surface of the ameba is of importance, for it widens to a very considerable extent the observational basis with which any theory of ameboid movement must conform. Since the properties of the outer layer are here described in detail for the first time, it becomes necessary to enquire to what extent the more commonly held theories of ameboid movement conform with the observed behavior of the surface film. Although the surface tension theory was the first detailed theory proposed toward an explanation of ameboid movement, I shall discuss Jennings' ('04) observations on the movements of the ameba first, because a great part of his work deals with the movements of the surface film, although he did not recognize it as distinct from the ectoplasm in its movements.

It is generally recognized that Dellinger's ('06) work proved that Jennings' conception of the ectoplasm as a permanent skin in which the ameba rolls along, is probably inadequate for such amebas as *proteus*; though singularly enough it is still supposed that *verrucosa* and its congeners move in the way described by Jennings (Hyman, '17, p. 83).

Jennings ('04) describes the movements of amebas, both *proteus* and *verrucosa* "types," as follows:

"In an advancing Amoeba substance flows forward on the upper surface, rolls over at the anterior edge, coming into contact with the substratum, then remaining quiet until the body of the ameba has passed over it. It then moves upward at the posterior end, and forward again on the upper surface, continuing in rotation as long as the ameba continues to progress. The motion of the upper surface is congruent with that of the endosarc, the two forming a single stream (p. 148).

"We have demonstrated above, for Amoeba at least, that the forward movement is not confined to a thin outer layer, but extends from the outer surface to the endosarc; in other words that the outer surface moves in continuity with the internal substance (p. 150).

"There is no regular transformation of endosarc into ectosarc at the anterior end. On the contrary the ectosarc here retains its continuity unbroken, moving across the anterior end in the same manner as across other parts of the body. In the same way the ectosarc is not regularly transformed into endosarc in the hinder part of the body.... Such transformation is by no means a regular accompaniment of locomotion" (p. 174).

According to Jennings, locomotion is aided by the projection of waves of hyaloplasm at the anterior edge, "an active movement of the protoplasm of a sort which has not been physically explained." These waves, attaching themselves to the substratum, enable the ameba to pull itself along by a rolling movement as described in the quotation above.

As to the rate of movement of the outer surface as compared with that of the endoplasm, Jennings concluded:

"The direction of movement of particles on the outer surface is the same as that of the underlying particles of endosarc. The rate is also about the same as for the endosarc, though often, or perhaps usually, the outer particles move a little more slowly than those in the endosarc" (p. 142).

In view of the observations recorded in the preceding pages it is clear that Jennings' statement that substance after moving forward on the upper surface, rolls over the anterior edge is quite erroneous. The attached particles, if heavy, may do so, but the surface film itself does not. It is, on the contrary, taken into the interior at the anterior edge.

The statement that the movement of the outer surface is congruent with that of the ectoplasm can likewise not be substantiated by observation, as has been demonstrated in the preceding pages. It is difficult to distinguish between the ectoplasm and the surface layer in such amebas as *sphaeronucleosus* and *verrucosa*, for there are no large crystals or other bodies which get caught in the ectoplasm as it is formed from endoplasm at the anterior end. But attentive observation will demonstrate very definitely that the ectoplasm here is stationary to the same degree as in *proteus*. The stationary properties of the ectoplasm are however not properly a matter for discussion; for five minutes' observation of a *proteus, discoides, annulata*, particularly a *laureata*, under 300 diameters magnification, will convince anyone that the ectoplasm is stationary while the surface film, with attached particles, moves over it. No one can possibly come to any other conclusion. Jennings' conclusion was due undoubtedly to an error of observation.

Jennings' statement that the rate of movement of the outer surface is the same as that of the endoplasm (p. 142) when taken in connection with his other statement that the ectoplasm is a more or less permanent skin, presents a mechanical impossibility; for unless the outer surface moves *twice as fast* as the endoplasm, no rolling movement would be possible. Several of Jennings' figures (especially Figures 38, 39, and 41) indicate in fact that he conceived of the outer surface as moving faster than the ameba advances, or that the upper surface moves *over the ameba* as the ameba moves over the substrate. Jennings' theory requires that the surface layer move twice as fast as the ameba advances. Hyman ('17) also makes a similar mistake in referring to the rate of movement of the outer surface (p. 85).

Lest the discussion of this point be suspected of being merely verbalistic, it should be recalled that the surface layer of *proteus* often moves at about the *same rate* as the ameba; that the surface layer of *discoides* moves about *twice as fast* as the ameba; that the surface layer of *verrucosa* and *sphaeronucleosus* moves about *three times as fast* as the ameba; and that the ectoplasm does not move at all. It is of course incumbent on one to discuss what is stated; one is not at liberty to select one of several possible interpretations.

To illustrate this point graphically so as to avoid as far as possible future confusion Figure 29 is appended. In *a* is shown a particle traveling on an ameba at the same rate of speed as the ameba; at *b* is shown a particle that moves twice as fast as the ameba; at *c* the attached heavy particle does not move at all. For the sake of completeness *d*, Figure 29, is added here. It illustrates the backward moving ectoplasm in an ameba that is suspended in a jelly medium that prevents the ameba from sinking to the bottom. It must be admitted that in thus considering the rate of movement of the various tissues of the ameba from a single standpoint, a point outside of the ameba, little room is left for confusion.

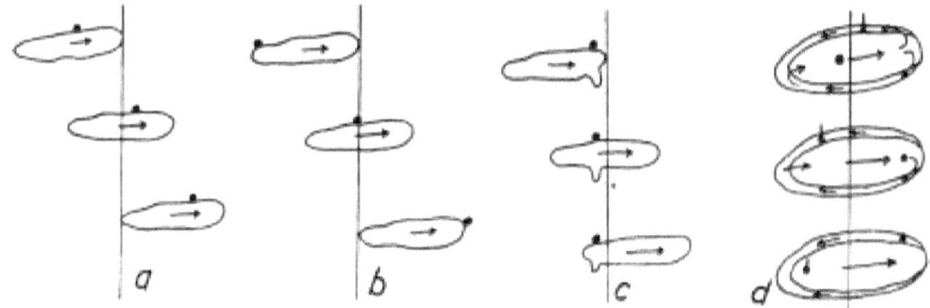

FIGURE 29.

a, a particle attached to an ameba and moving at the same rate as the ameba. This condition is often observed in *proteus* where the surface film, owing to its destruction during the formation of the longitudinal ridges, retards the forward movement of this layer. *b*, a particle attached to the surface film of an ameba moving twice as fast as the ameba. This condition is seen in *discoides, verrucosa, sphaeronucleosus*, etc. *c*, a particle on an ameba that does not move at all although the ameba does. This is seen when a heavy particle is laid on an ameba, too heavy for the surface film to move. *d*, movement of ectoplasm in an ameba suspended in a jelly medium. The vertical lines are to be considered as stationary.

There is comparatively little friction, if any at all, between the upper surface and the endosarc, according to Jennings' view, since both these layers move at the same rate and as a single stream. On the other hand there must be very considerable friction between the endoplasm and the lower ectoplasm, which does not move at all. This difference in the amount of friction must show itself in the different speeds of the endoplasm near the upper ectoplasm and near the lower ectoplasm. Observation indicates however that the most rapid streaming of the endoplasm is in the middle of the ameba or pseudopod and that it gradually becomes slower as the ectoplasm is approached on *all sides*.

We said above that if the ectoplasm were a more or less permanent skin in which the ameba rolled as described by Jennings, the upper surface (=ectosarc, Jennings), according to a well known mechanical principle, would have to move ahead about twice as fast as the ameba advances. Now the upper surface of *sphaeronucleosus* and of *verrucosa* in locomotion was found to move from three to three and a half times as fast as the ameba (Chapter VII). In discussing movement in "*verrucosa* and its relatives" Jennings says "the essential features of the movement seem to be (1) the advance of a wave from the upper surface at the anterior edge; (2) the pull exercised by this wave on the remainder of the upper surface of the body, bringing it forward. Most of the other phenomena follow as consequences of these two" (p. 146). Thus the amount of *stretch* of the upper surface would exceed the amount of *pull* on it from 50% to 75%!

Jennings' explanation of ameboid movement in which the important factor is a more or less permanent ectoplasm in which the ameba rolls along, would unquestionably produce rotary currents. Rhumbler ('98) recognized this and after full consideration rejected the idea that the ectoplasm is a permanent skin in which the ameba rolls along in locomotion, because rotary currents are not observed in a moving ameba. Anyone who doubts that rotary currents would be produced under these conditions can convince himself by putting a quantity of glycerine and some shavings in a large transparent rubber balloon or celloidin bag and letting it roll slowly down an incline in front of a strong light. If not too much glycerine is placed in the balloon, the shape of an ameba is closely enough approximated, and the rotary currents—down at the posterior and up at the anterior end—are well shown.

From all these considerations it is quite clear that Jennings' explanation of ameboid movement as a rolling movement can not any longer be maintained. His "discussion of this matter (the rolling movement hypothesis) is an excellent example of the fact that acumen and excellent reasoning may lead one astray in scientific matters when the observational basis for the reasoning is not secure." (These are Jennings' own words in criticism of Rhumbler on the same subject!)

The surface tension theory, with its many modifications, has had a great many more adherents than any other theory that has been advanced to explain ameboid movement. It represents the attempt of biologists to explain a vital phenomenon on physical grounds. The fact that it has been held to go further in this direction than any other, and the fact of its greater simplicity, doubtless are responsible for its wider acceptance. The recent criticism to which this theory has been subjected, however, indicates clearly enough that this theory does not really give a very adequate idea of the processes involved in ameboid movement after all, and in so far as feeding processes are concerned, the theory does not seem to apply at all according to Schaeffer ('16, '17). But it could hardly have been anything more than excellent guesswork if the surface tension theory *as advanced* by a number of writers had been found adequate, for the observational basis was very narrow, as the preceding pages have shown, and as the succeeding pages further show.

Not anything like a complete historical account of this theory with its numerous modifications will be attempted here. It would be a large undertaking, for nearly every biologist and biochemist has expressed himself on the subject. It does not appear that much is gained by merely recording the opinions, even of biologists, unless they are based on experimental or observational data, preferably their own. Scientific questions are not decided by ballot vote, and it is not apparent what value such a record of opinions would have except the doubtful one of showing whether the persons involved declared for or against the surface tension theory. Moreover such an account would not be interesting reading for those who want to know first of all what amebas can do. Only the more important modifications of the surface tension theory as applied to ameboid movements will therefore be discussed and these modifications will be considered important in proportion to the amount of observation or experiment on which they are based.

Attention has already been called in Chapter II to Berthold's ('86) theory of ameboid movement, which was the first attempt to explain this phenomenon on physical principles. As will be remembered, Berthold thought that the nature of the ameba's immediate environment determined when and in what direction it should move, the source of the energy of movement being supposed to be a decrease in the tension of the surface film of the ameba, brought about by some factor in the ameba's immediate environment.

One of the most elaborate attempts that has been made toward explaining ameboid movement on the basis of surface tension phenomena was that of Bütschli ('92). From his extensive knowledge of the lower organisms, especially the protozoa, he concluded that protoplasm is an emulsion of two fluids: a more concentrated "plasma," insoluble in water; and a thinner fluid, "enchylema." Ameboid movement was brought about by migration of enchylema droplets to the surface of the ameba at the anterior end, where they burst and spread over the surface, lowering its tension. The effect of this change in tension was held to be a flowing backward of the surface of the ameba and a flowing forward of the endoplasm. This is what happens in a drop of fluid, such as oil, on water to one side of which is brought a soapy solution. Bütschli described many experiments with fluids on which the surface tension was changed by appropriate means to simulate the process of movement. After Bütschli had developed his surface tension theory of movement, he discovered, as has already been noted, that in a pelomyxa the surface layer moves forward instead of backward as required by the surface tension theory. In spite of this however he still maintained that his theory of movement could be modified to apply to amebas generally, although so far as I have been able to find, he did not then or subsequently state how. From this we may infer that Bütschli himself probably concluded that the surface tension theory of movement as he developed it, is not of general application or is nothing more than a step in the development of such a theory.

Rhumbler has written a number of papers on the mechanics of ameboid movement, most of which are concerned with elaborations and modifications of a surface tension theory very similar to Bütschli's. Rhumbler published a general outline of his theory in 1898. The transformation of endoplasm into ectoplasm at the anterior end, and the reverse process at the posterior end, was stated to be an important part of his theory of movement, but just how this was necessary to surface tension effects was not explained in physical terms. Feeding was assumed to be caused by the direct action of the food body on the surface layer (ectoplasm) of the ameba. The presence of the food body, he held, produced a lowering of the surface tension of the ameba thus causing the ameba to flow around it ('98, p. 207). Subsequently, however, he ('14) came to the conclusion that many amebas cannot have fluid surfaces as usually understood, since they do not spread as a film over water when they come into contact with the surface. From this and other observations Rhumbler concluded ('14, pp. 501-514) that the surfaces of amebas are not to be compared with surface tension films on drops of inert simple fluids; but with the surface films of emulsions which take on the properties of a solid. Since the question of ameboid movement is not especially discussed in this later paper, it may be assumed that in this respect his ('98, '10) earlier views have not been materially modified. Rhumbler has suggested a great many physical models for the explanation of various ameboid activities such as feeding, defecation, movement and so forth.

In general agreement with Bütschli and Rhumbler were Verworn ('92), Blochmann ('94), Bernstein ('00), Jensen ('01, '02), and recently Hirschfeld ('09) and McClendon ('12). All these authors held that ameboid movement is a surface tension phenomenon. The application of the surface tension theory in explaining ameboid movement demands a fluid surface and a fluid interior and it is perhaps unnecessary to add that Bütschli, Rhumbler and the others mentioned held that the protoplasm is fluid. The question as to whether protoplasm is a fluid or possessed of an internal structure was however hotly debated and we find Fleming ('96), Heidenhain ('98), Klemensievicz ('98), Dellinger ('06) and others opposing the group of authors just mentioned, by contending that the streaming protoplasm must have some kind of structure. This question no longer concerns us however, owing to our rapidly increasing knowledge of colloidal solutions, for it is undoubtedly correct to hold that protoplasm is colloidal.

We have already insisted (p. 46) that the problem of ameboid movement is made more difficult by narrowing it down to the movements of ameba, and that to see the problem in its fullest aspect requires consideration of streaming protoplasm wherever found. Now it happens that there is in certain respects greater diversity of streaming to be found in plant cells than in animal cells, and it is not surprising therefore that explanations of streaming and ameboid movement have taken a different direction among botanists than among zoologists. It is for this reason doubtless that Ewart ('03), while espousing the surface tension theory as explaining streaming, does not look to the superficial surface of a plant cell as the source of the necessary energy, but to the interior of the protoplasm. This idea is, of course not entirely original with Ewart, for Bütschli, as we saw, believed that protoplasm has an emulsoid structure; but according to Bütschli's hypothesis, the surface forces were not brought into play in movement until the droplets of enchylema spread over the surface and so reduced the tension. Ewart, however points out that there is very much more surface energy present in the interior of streaming protoplasm than is required for all the movements known to protoplasm, including muscular contraction. According to Ewart's hypothesis the emulsion globules (disperse phase) have their surface tension lowered at corresponding points by electrical currents traversing the endoplasm, the electrical currents themselves originating in chemical actions.

While all available evidence from the study of colloidal solutions and from observation from protoplasm confirms Ewart's statement that more than sufficient energy is available in the interior of colloids for all purposes of movement, there is little or no evidence that the proper electrical currents are present to release or transform the surface energy into that of movement. This step in his explanation is therefore highly hypothetical and at present unconvincing. Moreover, this step in the theory would not be applicable to streaming as observed in amebas, without very considerable modification.

Recently Hyman ('17) has developed the surface tension theory of movement in the direction indicated by Ewart. The motive power is supposed to have its source in the contractility of the ectoplasm. The endoplasm is held to be a passive stream, not an active stream as Ewart supposed to be the case in plant cells. The power of contractility is held to be due to the process of gelation of endoplasm into ectoplasm, which is due to a change of phase, the fluid part of the endoplasm becoming dispersed and thereby developing surface energy in proportion as the amount of surface of the fluid is increased. This increase of surface produces the phenomenon of contractility.

Miss Hyman is wrong however when she says (p. 90) that the withdrawal and contraction of pseudopods are processes of gelation. This is clearly a physical impossibility, for the ectoplasm of the withdrawing pseudopod must become liquified into endoplasm, before it can be withdrawn. All writers excepting Jennings and Hyman are agreed on the continual transformation of ectoplasm into endoplasm at the posterior end while the reverse process goes on at the anterior end; and Hyman herself states (p. 89) that new ectoplasm is formed as the growing pseudopods extend into the water. So there must be liquefaction of the ectoplasm in withdrawing pseudopods, or very soon the whole ameba would be transformed into ectoplasm. As was shown in the preceding pages, liquefaction of the ectoplasm at the posterior end goes on at the same rate as gelation of the endoplasm at the anterior end. But at another place Hyman says:

"In fact according to Jennings, Dellinger, Gruber, and Schaeffer the surface of the ectoplasm actually flows forward at about the same rate as the forward advance, and this indicates that the advancing ectoplasm at the tip of the pseudopodium is derived from the surface ectoplasm and not from a transformation of endoplasm into ectoplasm at the end of the pseudopodium as Rhumbler supposed" (p. 89).

This quotation is not strictly accurate. Jennings says: "The pseudopodium grows chiefly from the base, so that any part of the surface retains nearly its original distance from the tip" (p. 156). Dellinger in a general way confirmed Jennings' conclusions. Gruber concluded that the outer layer was gelatinous, not protoplasmic. Schaeffer held the third layer to be extremely thin, "too thin to be seen easily," so it is impossible that the ectoplasm at the tip of a pseudopod, the thickness of which is readily seen, can be derived from the surface film.

The main conclusion however in Miss Hyman's paper is that there exists a metabolic gradient in the pseudopods of advancing amebas, the highest rate of metabolism being at the tip and the lowest at the base, for any one pseudopod. This conclusion is bound to be of the first importance in the explanation of ameboid movement. It will give our first real insight into the chemistry of ameboid movement. The fact that her method of demonstrating gradients has yielded uniform results in the hands of Child ('15), who originated it, as well as in her own when applied to a great many different organisms, entitles her conclusions to careful examination.

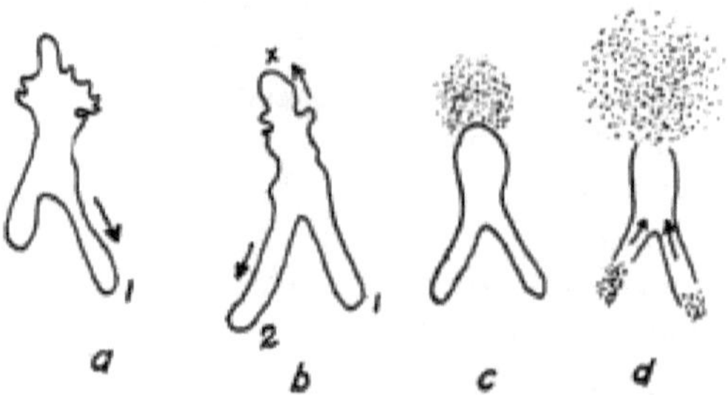

FIGURE 30.

Disintegration of an ameba in ¼ molecular KNC. After Hyman.
a, ameba flowing in the direction of the arrow. *b*, the ameba has
abandoned pseudopod 1 and flows into pseudopod 2, which has
become reactivated. The ameba was exposed to KNC at this stage
and, as is usual in such experiments, the posterior end at *x* becomes active. *c*, the youngest pseudopod, at *x*, disintegrated first.
d, the next youngest pseudopod, 2, disintegrated next. Pseudopod
1, the oldest, disintegrated last.

Of the observations there can be no doubt, for in many details earlier observations are confirmed. Her figures show that the tips of the pseudopods disintegrate
first in the potassium cyanide solution and later the regions further back (Figure
30). The question is, what causes the gradient of disintegration, which Miss Hyman takes to represent also a metabolic gradient? Where is the gradient located:
in the ectoplasm or in the endoplasm; or is the gelation process synonymous with
the metabolism that gives rise to the observed gradient? Miss Hyman does not say;
but it cannot be in the endoplasm, for it is in motion along the whole pseudopod
at about the same rate and it undergoes a demonstrable and visible change only
at the anterior end of the pseudopod. While metabolic changes might be higher at
the free end of the pseudopod, therefore, there would not be a gradient from there
on back. No recorded observations on the endoplasm along the length of a pseudopod can be arranged so as to form a gradient which would suggest a similar
gradient in metabolic rate; and if the endoplasm is a passively moved fluid as Hyman's theory seems to imply, a metabolic gradient would seem to be precluded.

In the ectoplasm however there exists a time gradient; that at the base of a
pseudopod is older than that near the tip, and observation generally tends to confirm the view that the older it is the firmer it becomes. This gradient in the amount
or extent of gelation corresponds with the disintegration gradient of cyanide along
a forming pseudopod. That is, the rate of disintegration is proportional to the age
of the ectoplasm. There is however no good evidence that the age of ectoplasm corresponds to the rate of metabolism, so that the younger the ectoplasm is the higher
will be the metabolic rate in it. The following statement seems to bear this out: "As
soon as the pseudopodium extends into the water its surfaces gelatinizes because
of contact with the water" (Hyman, '17, p. 89). Gelation is, according to Hyman,

a passive process and therefore not distinctively metabolic. She continues: "It is necessary therefore for the continuous production of a pseudopodium, that the metabolic change which is the cause of the liquefaction should continue to occur at the pseudopodial tip. There is thus produced the metabolic gradient along the pseudopodium which I have described...."

But if the metabolic gradient is bound up with the process of liquefaction, it is difficult to see how there can be a *gradient* along the pseudopod, for liquefaction takes place only at the tip, according to her own statement. As a matter of fact, however, *gelation* is constantly occurring at the tip of the pseudopod and to a less degree back along the sides of the pseudopod. Liquefaction occurs only at the posterior end of the ameba in orderly movement.

We must conclude therefore that while Hyman's data are of the first importance in contributing to the structure and behavior of the ameba, her contention that a metabolic gradient is demonstrated in the ameba is not convincing.

From this short account of the main theories that have been advanced to explain ameboid movement it appears that of the modern theories the only one that has been capable of adjusting itself to new investigations and observations is the surface tension theory. The earlier theories under this head were mistaken however in looking to the superficial film of the ameba as the source of energy. But with the increase in knowledge of the chemistry of colloids, the source of the surface energy came to be located in the interfaces between the phases of the colloidal system. As has already been remarked, there is more than sufficient free energy here to account for all the movements observed in protoplasm; there remains the problem of explaining how the surface energy is transformed into that of movement. As Graham ('61) remarked: "The colloidal is in fact a dynamical state of matter. The colloid possesses *energia*. It may be looked upon as the probable primary source of the force (energy) appearing in the phenomena of vitality."

Now, viewing streaming wherever it occurs in the protoplasm of animals or plant cells the surface tension theory, as far as observations permit, applies to the various conditions of streaming as follows.

In the first place we shall begin with the assumption that is generally held, that protoplasm is a reversible colloidal solution consisting mainly of proteins, with some carbohydrates, lipoids, etc., on the one hand and water on the other. Its reversibility consists of course in being able to change from a sol to a gel state and the reverse, the water being in the disperse phase in the gel state. The consistency of the protoplasm therefore depends upon two factors: upon the amount of water present, and upon the degree of its dispersion; the smaller the droplets the more solid will be the gel because of the increase in surface of the mass. Colloids exhibit the property of contractility in proportion as the droplets of water are decreased in size; or, which amounts to the same thing, in proportion as the amount of the surface of the water is increased. It appears as if the source of energy of contractility was the free energy in the surface films of the internal phase of the gel.

Taking the amebas as a group and applying these principles of colloidal solutions, we find that we can arrange the amebas in a series of four or more grades representing differences of fluidity of the protoplasm. Among the most fluid are *Amoeba limicola* and *Pelomyxa schiedti*; in the next group, with less fluid protoplasm is *Amoeba dubia*; in the third group is *A. proteus* and *A. discoides*; in the fourth group, with the least fluid protoplasm, come *A. radiosa* and *A. verrucosa*. These groups represent a progressive increase in the amount of ectoplasm in proportion to the endoplasm. There being less water present in the higher groups than in the lower, which follows from a stiffer endoplasm, it is possible for them to form endoplasm, that is, to change phase, more readily. And as a corollary to this we may add that more pseudopods are formed, since ectoplasm can be formed more readily. (The *verrucosa* types possess very stiff ectoplasm, and they increase their surface by flattening out and by forming longitudinal ridges. They cannot for some unknown reason form pseudopods). Again with the increase in the consistency of the protoplasm, the pseudopods become more slender (and stiffer) and more contractile, the most slender pseudopods (*radiosa, flagellipodia*) being very much more contractile than the larger ones of *proteus* or *discoides*, for example. An additional factor operates here, however, for some of the slender pseudopods as of *radiosa* and *bilzi* are static and for a great part of their existence practically incapable of contraction. The high development of contractility follows, of course, from the high degree of dispersion of the internal phase in ectoplasm, of which these pseudopods almost wholly consist. Thus, many, if not most, of the more generalized peculiarities of form of amebas may be traced to the amount of water in the protoplasm.

The number of pseudopods in an ameba is an important factor in its method of locomotion, as may readily be perceived. Since amebas generally move with great variation in speed as one compares the different species, whether they form very little ectoplasm or very much, and are able to maintain themselves on their paths, it follows that ectoplasm formation by itself does not play an important part in originating movement. But it requires only a few minutes' observation to see that ectoplasm is necessary to guide the ameba, so to speak, and to make the endoplasmic stream effective for the purpose of orderly movement. It requires very little imagination to see what would happen if no ectoplasm were present in a *limicola* or any very fluid ameba. Streaming would undoubtedly occur as before, but the currents would be rotational and irregular and no progression could take place. The ectoplasm furnishes just that stiff tube against which the backward action of the endoplasm can impinge so to speak in order to enable it to flow forward. The ectoplasm is essential for orderly movement forward, but it is not essential for streaming.

But this does not imply that the contractile power of the ectoplasm may not be used to aid in propelling the endoplasm in streaming. It has been demonstrated by Miss Hyman ('17) that the ectoplasm is actually contractile when the ameba is strongly stimulated all over its exterior by a solution of potassium cyanide. While this proves only the contractile powers of the ectoplasm under exceptional conditions, and when at rest, it is not impossible that under ordinary conditions of locomotion it may aid in streaming. There is however one observation which may, upon further investigation, negative this possibility. Frequently in a pseudopod about to be retracted some of the endoplasm flows toward the tip while the rest flows toward the base (Figure 1, p. 11).

One more point needs mention in this connection, and that is the small waves of clear protoplasm which are thrown out by many amebas at their anterior ends during locomotion. They are especially prominent in *A. bigemma* (Figure 7) and in *radiosa* (Figure 8), but they are formed in perhaps all species. Observation does not indicate that they move in exactly the same way as the main body of the endoplasm, even if the larger granules could be left out of account. They behave more like the clear pseudopods of *Difflugia* and *Arcella* and the foraminifera.

Although these waves are frequently not to be seen during locomotion in *Amoeba proteus* and other large amebas, particularly in *Pelomyxa palustris* and *P. belevskii*, it is possible that the wave forming process has become indistinguishably merged with endoplasmic streaming. It is not impossible that the projection of these waves is the purest expression of ameboid movement. But on account of their small size and transparency, it is very much more difficult to investigate them than streaming of the granular endoplasm, as it is observed in amebas, ciliates and plant cells. It seems to be true however that streaming can occur in the entire absence of these waves, so their importance in ameboid movement is probably secondary.

CHAPTER X

STREAMING, CONTRACTILITY AND AMEBOID MOVEMENT

The nearest relatives of the amebas are the shelled rhizopods, the Difflugias and the Arcellas and their congeners. The movement of these organisms is quite different from that of the amebas in that the whole body of the endoplasm does not stream into the pseudopods, but only a small portion of it. There is consequently no regular transformation of ectoplasm into endoplasm at the posterior end, that is, the protoplasmic mass within the shell. The method of movement in *Difflugia* was described by Dellinger ('06). A pseudopod is thrown out to a considerable distance. It fastens itself to the substrate at the tip. It then contracts, pulling the *Difflugia* forwards. While this pseudopod is contracting, another one is extended in the same direction. When it has arrived at the maximum length, it fastens itself at the tip and then contracts, pulling the *Difflugia* along. Continued locomotion consists of a repetition of this process. The pseudopods are slender and consist nearly always of clear protoplasm. Only occasionally does one see conspicuous endoplasmic granules flow into a pseudopod, and then only at the base.

The transparency of the pseudopods in *Difflugia* and the absence of granules in the protoplasm composing them, prevents one from seeing clearly how the pseudopods are formed, that is, whether or not there is a regular transformation of endoplasm into ectoplasm at the anterior end. The fact that one occasionally sees the endoplasm stream into the base of a pseudopod in the same way as was described for ameban pseudopods, indicates that the method of formation of pseudopods in *Difflugia* is in general similar to that in ameba. But the process is not exactly the same, for the surface layer on the pseudopods of *Difflugia* does not move as fast as the tips of the pseudopods advance, while in amebas the surface layer moves faster than the pseudopods. What this difference indicates has not yet been ascertained.

The protoplasm of the pseudopods of *Difflugia* is thick and the power of contractility highly developed, for the pseudopods readily move about in the water like a tentacle. The demarcation line between ectoplasm and endoplasm is very difficult to see, consequently no definite idea can be given as to the thickness of the ectoplasm. When a pseudopod is being extended the whole contents seem to move at about the same rate as the pseudopod advances, differing thus from amebas, in the pseudopods of which the central core of the endoplasmic stream flows considerably faster than the tip of the pseudopod advances through the water. But when a large pseudopod is cut off from a *Difflugia* it is able to move after the manner of an ameba without a nucleus (Verworn, '94).

In heliozoans protoplasmic streaming is quite different from that in ameba or *Difflugia*. The pseudopods are usually straight, radiating from the central body. They possess usually a central axial rod of condensed or strongly gelatinized protoplasm around which is a layer of thick protoplasm with the properties of ectoplasm. Heliozoans for the most part move slowly; in fact many of them are pelagic and in these the power of locomotion on a solid substratum is very slow. There is however one species, *Acanthocystis ludibunda*, which, according to Penard ('04), can move twenty times its diameter in one minute by rolling. This illustrates a highly developed power of contractility in the pseudopods of this organism, for since only about one-fifth of the circumference can be in contact with the solid substratum, the pseudopods must attach themselves, contract so as to pull the *Acanthocystis* along, and relax their hold, all in the space of two seconds.

Among pseudopod forming organisms, the highest development of contractility is found in the foraminifera. As is well known, these organisms form finely anastomosing pseudopods which frequently cover the substratum with a network of protoplasmic strands. The terminal sections of these strands are frequently so thin and transparent that they cannot be seen easily with the microscope. As a rule the granular endoplasm is observable only in the main body of the organism and in the larger trunks of the pseudopods. Much the larger part of the pseudopods, as measured lineally, is devoid of granular endoplasm. The great power of contractility and the speed with which contraction may occur in *Biomyxa*, a fresh water foraminifer, have already been mentioned (Figure 12, p. 47). Similar observations have been recorded by other observers, recently by Schultz ('15), who compares the contractility of foraminiferan pseudopods to that of rubber bands. In fact as one watches the movements of a *Biomyxa*, for example, under moderately high magnification, one gains the impression that there seems to be no restriction imposed upon the extent of contractility in the pseudopods. They seem to possess perfect elasticity. As to the transformation of endoplasm into ectoplasm, little can be said, owing to the transparency of the protoplasm. But the whole of the pseudopod, when forming, seems to stream forward. As in *Difflugia*, the interior streams flow at about the same rate as the pseudopod as a whole advances. The highly developed power of contractility however demands rapid changes in phase of the colloidal system, and also a thick consistency. The behavior of pieces of the pseudopodial network, when cut from a *Biomyxa*, shows clearly that the protoplasm is actually thick, as compared with that of an *Amoeba proteus*. When a *Biomyxa* is contracted into a spherical mass, the interior exhibits continual rapidly streaming movements. Some of these are rotational but most of them are radial. All of the streams frequently change their direction and extent. No corresponding changes are visible in the outer peripheral layer.

Among plants, some of the algae possess ameboid protoplasts at one stage or another of their life cycle, but the details of streaming have not been made out. It has been reported however that the zoospores of some parasitic fungi move to all appearances exactly like small amebas. We likewise lack details of the streaming of the myxomycete plasmodia. From a more or less cursory examination of a small aquatic plasmodium of undetermined species, it appeared that the formation of pseudopods and the process of streaming were quite different from similar processes in the foraminifera. The pseudopods do not act independently as in foraminifera. At almost the same moment the protoplasm begins to flow from the pseudopods in a large section of the plasmodium and into another section; then soon thereafter the protoplasm flows back again. This oscillatory streaming is continued presumably as long as the myxomycete is in the plasmodial stage. With every change in the direction of movement of streaming, there is produced, however, a change in the shapes of the pseudopods, so that with a number of oscillations in streaming an appreciable degree of locomotion is effected. The direction of locomotion can be markedly affected by changes in light intensity and moisture distribution, as shown by the observations of Baranetzsky ('76), Stahl ('84) and others, but just how these changes in the direction of locomotion were produced is not recorded. There is a definite ectoplasm and a definite endoplasm in the myxomycete plasmodia, but the details of their transformations, the one into the other, have not been determined; but since the surface layer is stationary, it is probable that there is no such regular transformation of endoplasm into ectoplasm at the anterior ends of pseudopods as there is in ameba. But this phase of the subject needs further investigation before any conclusions can be drawn. The power of contractility is present, but apparently only to a slight degree. Too little is known of the streaming process in these organisms to compare it in detail with the same phenomenon in rhizopods.

The streaming of protoplasm in plants has received a good deal of attention, though only comparatively little experimental work has been done. Streaming is observed in a great many plant cells, and in some cells such as the large internodal cells of *Chara* and *Nitella*, the process may be easily observed. The essential features of a plant cell in which streaming occurs are, first, the external cell wall of cellulose, which of course prevents any change of shape in the cell such as is observed in naked protoplasts as, for example, ameba. Inside of the cell wall is a layer of ectoplasm which has essentially the same properties as the ectoplasm of amebas. In some cells such as those of *Chara*, the ectoplasmic layer is thick and contains nearly all the chloroplastids, while in the leaf cells of *Elodea* the ectoplasm is extremely thin and is practically free from chloroplastids. In the interior of the cell are found the streaming endoplasm and one or more large vacuoles filled with cell sap.

The streaming is of two types which are often distinguished from each other by the names *rotational* and *circulatory*. But the distinction seems to be of little significance, for the same cell may at different times show both types of streaming. When there is a single vacuole only in the cell, it occupies the center of the cell, and the endoplasm then rotates between it and the ectoplasm. Whenever there are strands of endoplasm flowing across the vacuole, the peripheral streaming is no longer rotational but it is then called circulatory. By external stimulation of the cell, Ewart ('03) was able to change circulatory streaming into rotational; that is, the numerous small streams traversing the cell sap in many directions were caused to retract into a single stream around the periphery of the cell. This change brought about a heightened velocity in streaming, showing that the small strands traversing the cell sap meet with some resistance. There is no essential difference between streaming in plant cells, whether rotational or circulatory, from the rotational streaming so commonly found in protozoa.

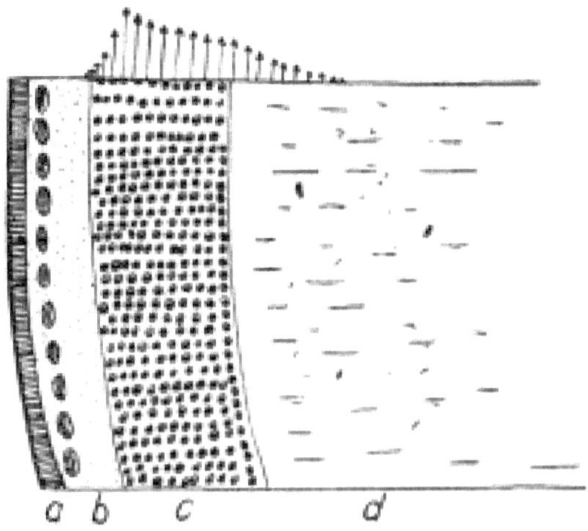

FIGURE 31.

Diagram of a section of a *Chara* cell showing rows of emulsion globules in the endoplasm, after Ewart. *a*, cell wall. *b*, ectoplasm. *c*, endoplasm, *d*, cell sap. The arrows at the top of the figure indicate by their lengths, the amount of movement of the endoplasm and cell sap in streaming.

Ewart has also observed that in the streaming of the endoplasm, there is a variation of velocity of streaming in different parts of the stream (Figure 31). The middle of the stream moves fastest while the layer near the ectoplasm moves very slowly and the layer in contact with the ectoplasm moves hardly at all. But the endoplasm in contact with the central vacuole moves only a little more slowly than the middle of the stream, and the effect of this is that the outer edge of the vacuole is dragged along with the moving endoplasm. This is an important observation and from it Ewart concludes that the energy which produces the streaming movement must be liberated, not at the boundary between the ectoplasm and the endoplasm, nor at that between the endoplasm and the vacuole, but within the endoplasmic stream itself. In this conclusion Ewart is undoubtedly correct, for as a physical phenomenon, no other conclusion is at present possible.

Other experiments made upon the velocity of streaming in plant cells indicate that the streaming process obeys the laws of physics. The velocity varies with the proportion of water present in the endoplasm,—the more water, the faster the streaming (Ewart, '03). The effect of temperature on streaming, noted first by Corti ('74), and studied by Velten, ('76), Schaeffer ('98), Ewart ('03) and other writers, is also such as would be expected if the endoplasm were a simple physical fluid.

The rotational streaming in plant cells, such as those of *Chara*, is very similar to the rotational streaming in paramecium and numerous other ciliates. In these organisms it is often called cyclosis. A paramecium differs, however, from a plant cell exhibiting rotational streaming in that no central vacuole is present. This space in paramecium is occupied by the gullet, the nucleus and some endoplasm which is not in the main stream. The effect of this difference seems to be one affecting velocity only, slowing it down, for in the *Chara* cell the endoplasm meets with much less friction when moving in contact with the vacuolar wall than when moving in contact with the ectoplasm. Its velocity is still further reduced by the large food vacuoles which are almost always carried by the endoplasm, for these vacuoles behave like solid bodies in the endoplasmic stream. During streaming these vacuoles are often seen coming close to the limiting ectoplasm, when they act as obstructions to the flow of the endoplasm. The velocity of the endoplasmic stream in paramecium is relatively slow, ten to twenty minutes being required for a complete revolution.

In *Frontonia leucas*, another large ciliate, rotational streaming is under the control of the organism, and special use is made of it in feeding. *Frontonia* feeds mostly, if not entirely, on large particles. It has no oral groove like paramecium has, and when swimming no ciliary vortex is produced such as is seen in paramecium. *Frontonia* feeds mostly by "browsing," that is by eating particles lying on or against some solid support, though it is able also to feed upon particles suspended in the water.

Oscillatoria and *Lyngbia* and other filamentous algae are the chief food of *Frontonia*. Filaments of these algae are ingested by pulling them into the mouth and then rolling them up into a coil in the body. Pieces of *Oscillatoria* six to eight times as long as the *Frontonia* are readily eaten in this way.

As a rule the end of a filament is seized by the mouth and gradually passed back into the body (Figure 32, *a*). As soon as the tip of the filament is well in the mouth and in contact with the endoplasm, streaming begins in the endoplasm in the region of the mouth and takes a direction directly back against the aboral wall, almost, if not quite perpendicular to the longitudinal axis. This stream of endoplasm carries the filament back to the aboral wall, sometimes pushing out the wall a considerable distance. Presently, however, the filament is carried posteriorly along the aboral wall by the streaming protoplasm, which has by this time become rotational, and after reaching the posterior end the filament is brought up along the oral wall. The rotational streaming continues until the entire filament is wound up, which in exceptional cases may make four or five coils inside the animal.

The mouth has considerable grasping power. This is shown in Figure 32 where a filament of *Oscillatoria* was bent upon itself by the mouth and then rolled up in the body by the endoplasm in the same manner as a single filament. The mere viscosity of the endoplasm would be insufficient to bring about the bending of the filament. For the sake of comparison it should be added that a similar grasping power is also present in paramecium. The moment the food vacuole at the mouth is large enough, the endoplasm pulls it away and moves it rapidly toward the posterior end of the paramecium, much more rapidly than it would be carried by the rotationally streaming endoplasm. But from the posterior end forward the food vacuole is carried at the same rate as are the other particles in the endoplasm. In both *Frontonia* and paramecium rapid endoplasmic streaming precedes for a short distance the forward end of the ingested filament or the food vacuole (Figure 32, *a*).

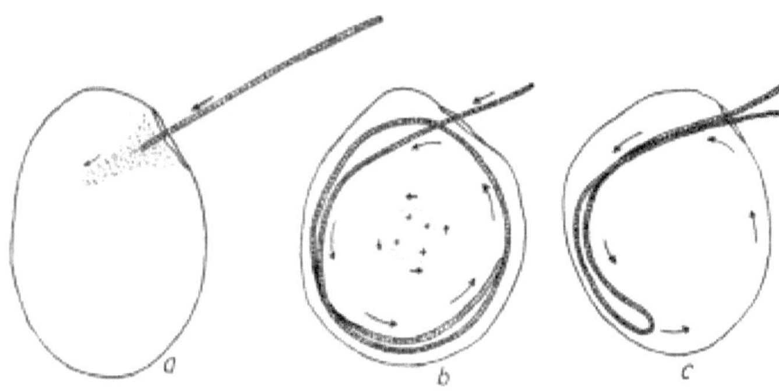

FIGURE 32.

Showing ingestion of alga filaments in *Frontonia leucas*. *a*, the beginning of the ingestion of an alga filament. Note the streaming of the endoplasm *preceding* the end of the filament. *b*, almost two complete coils of the filament have been rolled up inside the *Frontonia* by the rotary streaming endoplasm. The endoplasm in the center of the animal is stationary. *c*, a filament, if thin, may be grasped anywhere along its length, bent together and swallowed in the usual manner. Diameter of *a*, 250 microns.

If a filament of alga is too long for the *Frontonia*, or one end of it is fast, streaming is reversed after several coils have been rolled up and the filament is ejected. So far as could be observed, the streaming process is reversed in all details, though the rate of ejection seemed to be somewhat slower than the rate of ingestion. Occasionally, however, ejection is accomplished much more quickly. If there are several coils of a filament whose other end is fast, rolled up inside of a *Frontonia*, the mouth sometimes stretches antero-posteriorly until the coil as a whole without unwinding is thrown out of the body. The viscosity of the endoplasm might lead one to expect that some of the endoplasm would be brought out with the alga, but such is not the case.

The essential differences between rotational streaming in *Frontonia* and in paramecium are: (1) It is under the control of the organism in *Frontonia* while in paramecium it is a continuous reversible process. (2) It is much more rapid in *Frontonia* than in paramecium. On the other hand, the physics of streaming in both organisms is essentially the same, so far as could be detected. In both organisms the energy of streaming is liberated within the endoplasm. This is especially well shown in the first stages of feeding.

Besides these organisms in which streaming occurs, either in a part of the organism or the whole, streaming is also found to occur in a great variety of plants other than those already mentioned; in the leukocytes of perhaps all coelomates; in some animal egg cells, such as the sponges, hydra and molluscs; in pigment cells, especially in batrachians and lacertilians; in phagocytes and wandering cells of a great many animals; in the nuclei of some animal cells; and in the intestinal epithelial cells of perhaps all metazoans. In almost none of these cases however do we know more than the bare fact that streaming occurs. No details are known. Consequently in so far as the purposes of this book are concerned it will not be apropos to discuss these cases further except to record the thesis that there is no evidence tending to show that these cases are not at bottom all characterized by the operation of the same fundamental process.

In all these cases of animal and plant cells and tissues in which ameboid movement occurs the process of streaming is easily observed in all of them, but the phenomenon of contractility is not noticeable in some cells except under special conditions, while in other cells it is operating continually. This indicates that there are other factors at work in addition to mere phase changes in the colloidal system to produce now contractility, now streaming. A high power of contractility and of streaming are not present in the same mass of protoplasm at the same time, though these powers may both be present at different times (*Biomyxa*).

Contractility can be explained in a general (though not yet in a detailed) way as due to a change in phase, more or less complete, in the colloidal system which is held to be the chief characteristic of the physical aspect of protoplasm. The change of phase is of course, associated with a change in the amount of surface energy, which is the ultimate source of the energy of contractility.

Streaming, however, does not depend upon a *marked* change of phase resulting in gelation, for observation has failed to detect this process going on to any extent whatever in streaming protoplasm. Further, an increase in the amount of water in the protoplasm is associated with more rapid streaming. If streaming therefore depends upon a phase change in a colloidal system, it must be in the direction of liquefaction, that is, changing the internal more fluid phase to the external phase. A phase change in one direction would thus lead to contractility, while a change in the other direction would lead to streaming.

Theories accounting for the intimate nature of the process of streaming without special reference to ameboid movement, have been offered by many botanists. In most plant cells in which streaming movements occur the ectoplasmic covering does not change shape. Streaming of the endoplasm therefore is a much less complicated process in such a case than in an ameba where locomotion is also present. It is to be expected therefore that a theory of streaming based upon observation of a plant cell such as is found in *Chara* would be different from one based upon observation of a moving ameba. Such is found to be the case, as the following discussion of some of the principal theories accounting for streaming in plant cells strikingly shows.

(1) *The contractility theories.* Corti ('74), who was the first to record observations on the process of streaming in plants thought that the movement of the endoplasm

was caused by waves of contraction passing around the cell in a way analogous to that in which fluid may be passed through a rubber tube by closing the finger over it and passing it along the tube. Heidenhain ('63), Kühne ('64), Brücke ('64), Hanstein ('80), in one form or another also have expressed their adherence to the contractility theory. More recently Dellinger ('06, p. 356) postulated contractile fibrillae in rhizopods similar to those postulated by Brücke to explain protoplasmic streaming. The contractility theories are no longer considered tenable, for no waves of contractility can be demonstrated, as the theories of Corti, Heidenhain, et al. demand, and contractile fibers can neither be demonstrated nor can they be conceived to exist in endoplasm which exhibits all the essential properties of a fluid.

(2) *The imbibition theories.* Sachs ('65), Hoffmeister ('67) and Englemann ('79) conceived of streaming as being caused by certain constituents of the cell imbibing water and later discharging it. Sachs and Hoffmeister thought that waves of imbibition and extrusion of water passing progressively along the cell was able to cause movement of the protoplasm. Ewart ('03) has shown, however, that as much as 2000 times its own volume of water would have to be imbibed by a cell of *Nitella* in the course of a day to account for the amount of streaming observed, and that no sign of the extrusion of water could be detected by observing small suspended particles in the immediate vicinity of the cell. Englemann's theory involving a change of shape of his hypothetical supra-molecular "Inotagmas," by the imbibition of water and the subsequent release if it, which was supposed to account for the movement of the protoplasm while streaming, has been considered too hypothetical and too far removed from the realm of experiment to be of real value, either as an explanation or as a working hypothesis.

(3) *The oxidation theory of Verworn.* Verworn ('92, '09) has postulated a "Biogen Molecule" which exists only in living protoplasm and dissociates when protoplasm dies into a number of chemical molecules of albumin and other substances. Ameboid movement and streaming generally, according to Verworn, is caused by the lowering of the superficial surface tension in the moving mass of protoplasm followed by streaming of the protoplasm toward the point of lowered tension. The lowering of the surface tension is brought about by a union of the Biogen Molecule with oxygen. With the dissociation of the biogen-oxygen compound, presumably through a respiratory process, the surface tension rises again. This theory does not hold for amebas, for we saw in the preceding pages that the surface tension is higher at the anterior ends of pseudopods than elsewhere on the ameba. And in plants, as Ewart ('03) has shown, oxygen does not seem necessary to the streaming process, for the endoplasm of *Chara* cells continues to stream for many days in the entire absence of oxygen. It is possible that there would be enough loosely fixed oxygen in the endoplasm of *Chara* to supply the demands of Verworn's theory; but the very hypothetical nature of his theory prevents one from discussing this possibility.

(4) *The electrical theories.* These fall into three classes: (a) *The galvanic theory.* Amici ('18) suggested that the chloroplastids floating in the endoplasm of plant cells acted as galvanic cells, setting up currents in the endoplasm which in some

way caused the endoplasm to move. Dutrochet and Becquerel ('38) also held to this explanation. A fatal defect of this theory is that streaming occurs in a great variety of cells, myxomycete plasmodia, amebas, stamen hairs of *Tradescantia*, etc., in which no chloroplastids occur; and there is no ground for assuming that the causes of streaming in cells with chloroplastids is fundamentally different from that in other cells. (b) *The electromagnetic theory.* Velten ('72, '73) and Hörmann ('98) are chiefly responsible for the development of the electromagnetic theory. They hold that chloroplastids have an independent movement of their own; but the principal postulate of this theory is that there is electric repulsion between the ectoplasm and the endoplasm. Ewart ('03) has pointed out, however, that this theory is contradicted by the fact that when streaming becomes very active in *Elodea*, the ectoplasm becomes exceedingly thin and therefore would show movement in the direction opposite to that of the endoplasm if there were magnetic repulsion between these layers. Moreover, the formation of threads of endoplasm across the central vacuoles in plant cells, and the much branched network of pseudopods in plasmodia and foraminifera would be very difficult if not quite impossible to explain on this assumption. (c) *The electro-chemical surface-tension theory of Ewart.* As the result of a considerable amount of experiment and observation on endoplasmic streaming in plants, Ewart ('03) has come to the conclusion that there are differences in electrical potential between the protoplasm-vacuole boundary and the protoplasm-cell wall boundary, and that as a consequence electrical currents are passing between these points, traversing the protoplasmic stream. If now it is assumed that the particles in the endoplasm, which are electrically polarized, have the surface tension of their corresponding ends decreased when electric currents traverse the endoplasmic stream, the particles and, of necessity, the whole stream of endoplasm would move in the direction of lowered surface tension (Figure 31, p. 96). Continuous chemical actions would be necessary to maintain the conditions as outlined. This theory accords with the facts so far as it goes, but it does not explain the streaming in threads across the vacuole in the plant cell, thus necessitating two theories for the explanation of streaming within a single cell at the same moment. Moreover a central vacuole of cell sap seems always to be required to fulfill the conditions of this theory, and this, as is readily seen, makes it impossible to apply it to streaming in amebas, myxomycetes, foraminifera and ciliates.

The fundamental cause of streaming is therefore still to be discovered, for neither the theories of streaming as applied to ameba, nor those described above which refer especially to plant cells, are satisfactory. But a significant point in these theories is that with increasing information, they come more and more to demand a colloidal structure in the protoplasm. It is the surface energy in the interfaces in the colloidal system which comes to be regarded as the primary source of the energy. But all attempts thus far to explain exactly how this energy is utilized have been unsuccessful. Gaidukov's ('10) observation is of some interest, however in this connection. He found that the occasional stopping of streaming in cells of *Vallisneria* is accompanied by a cessation of Brownian movement, which indicates a change from a sol to a gel state. This proves therefore that colloidal changes are possible in streaming protoplasm, and that the general search for an explanation of streaming along this line is proceeding in the right direction. The researches of

Bancroft ('13, '14) and especially of Clowes ('13, '16) on the nature of the change of phase in emulsions are very instructive in this connection; and it is undoubtedly true that as rapid progress is now being made by the investigation of colloidal solutions as by the direct study of protoplasm, in solving the problem of streaming.

The problem of the *control* of the streaming process, which is of course much the most important feature of streaming, will probably be solved, at least in part, when the mechanics of streaming is understood.

CHAPTER XI

THE SURFACE LAYER AS A LOCOMOTOR ORGAN

The discussion of the surface film of ameba and its movements during loco-motion naturally led to a discussion of the various theories that have been offered to explain ameboid movement and protoplasmic streaming. Now the fact that the ameba possesses a traveling surface film which can carry particles recalls similar behavior in Oscillatorias and in the diatoms. No new observations have been made very recently, but by comparison of the behavior of particles carried by an Oscillatoria filament and by ameba, it is found that the nature of the movement, the rate of movement, the degree of adhesion of the particles, the sizes of the particles carried and so on, are similar in both organisms. This indicates that there is a surface layer on Oscillatoria threads that is similar to that which has been described in amebas, and whose movement is probably also effected by changes in surface extension; but just how this change is effected is not clear owing to the spiral path the particles take as they travel along the Oscillatoria filament. The spiral has an angle of about sixty degrees, which must be related in some way to the finer structure of the cells of which the filament is composed. The suggestion that movement is caused by the rapid and forcible exudation of mucus is exceedingly improbable if not physically impossible. It is difficult to see how the spiral direction of the flow of mucus could be brought about, to say nothing of the frequent change in direction of the flow. In a surface tension film, however, the direction of movement is readily determined by the location of the points where the tension is changed. Mucus secreting glands would need special structural devices such as secretory tubes bent at an angle to control the direction of flow, while no such structural devices are necessary if the propelling force is surface energy. In short, it is difficult to see how any movement at all could be produced by the act of secretion of mucus, while from what we have seen in the ameba, surface tension changes could easily produce movement in Oscillatoria. The spiral feature of the movement has no explanation that is based on observational data. It may be added here that the surface film in amebas is powerful enough to enable them to move by means of it. One sometimes sees *sphaeronucleosus* or small individuals of *verrucosa*, that are lying loose on the substratum, actively streaming, but moving slowly and more or less irregularly backwards. This movement is due to the activity of the surface film.

The suggestion that no extra-cellular protoplasmic layer has been demonstrated in Oscillatoria is not a cogent argument against the surface tension hypothesis, since the surface film would need to be but a small fraction of a micron thick, too thin to be demonstrated by histological methods now in vogue. It is also to be remembered that the surface film in ameba can be demonstrated in no other way at present than by its particle-carrying capacity.

The main features of the movements of diatoms are very similar to those of Oscillatoria. Müller ('89, '97, '99) has shown that the gliding movements of diatoms are not due to the ejection of water, but to the streaming of protoplasm on the outside of the shells. Foreign particles are carried by these shallow streams of protoplasm in quite the same manner as by the surface film of the ameba. And there seems to be no evidence against the assumption that these shallow streams, at least the surface films over them, owe their movement to changes in surface tension.

Desmids also glide about slowly, leaving a track of mucus behind. Only one explanation for locomotion has been advanced, and that is that it is due to the secretion of mucus (Klebs, '85). This explanation is likely to be as wide of the mark as the similar explanation in the case of Oscillatoria. There is no question concerning the excretion of mucus, but the source of the locomotive energy is probably here also surface energy, though the observational data are too few to try to locate the regions where the changes in tension occur.

It has been a matter of considerable surprise to me to find that the so-called "crawling" euglenas, in addition to the diatoms, desmids, Oscillatoria, Beggiatoa and perhaps other forms of life such as the Gregarinidas, also possess extra-cellular films which carry particles as do amebas and Oscillatoria, and move about through the agency of this film. The film travels spirally around the euglena as it does in Oscillatoria filaments. In at least two species the film moves parallel to the spiral striations on the outer surface. In one species no spiral striations could be detected, although the film moved spirally. The species of euglenas in which these movements were observed, were not identified.

The character of the movement of the euglenas is very similar to that of the diatoms excepting that most of the diatoms do not revolve on their longitudinal axes. The movement of particles on the surface film of euglenas is quite like that in Oscillatoria, though it is only under exceptional circumstances that one can see particles attached to the surface film. The movement of the particles indicates that the surface film moves from the anterior end toward the posterior end, but whether the "spine" is to be included was not definitely determined. The degree of cohesiveness of the film is high, for locomotion is rapid, even if only a small part of the posterior end is in contact with the substratum, as when moving over an Oscillatoria filament. To one who has seen the movements of the surface films of amebas, diatoms and Oscillatorial filaments, the most reasonable conclusion seems to be that the cause of locomotion in crawling euglenas is the same as that in Oscillatoria and diatoms.

Evidence contributing to this conclusion is found in the circumstance that crawling euglenas, diatoms and Oscillatoria threads are much more refractory to galvanic currents than flagellate euglenas or other flagellates or ciliates: The electrical apparatus at my disposal was rather crude, but I was unable to find that I could influence the direction or character of movement of Oscillatoria filaments, diatoms or crawling euglenas without injuring the organisms. Currents which had produced a marked effect on ciliates or flagellates produced no effect whatever on amebas, diatoms, Oscillatoria or crawling euglenas. Diatoms are particularly resistant to the effect of electrical currents.

The general conclusion regarding the source of energy of the moving surface films, whether found on amebas, diatoms, desmids, or crawling euglenas, is that all derive their motive power from the energy in the superficial films of these organisms; while ameboid streaming, if it is a surface tension phenomenon as seems to be the case, depends upon the surface energy of the interfaces of the emulsoid colloidal system in the endoplasm. It has already been seen that those cases of locomotion due in large measure to the power of contractility in the ectoplasm (Difflugia, Foraminifera) are also explained as being due to a change of phase in the colloidal system, which is in itself a surface tension effect. It appears therefore that all the lower organisms that move, excepting flagellated or ciliated organisms (of whose motor mechanism we have no detailed knowledge), depend upon surface energy as the source of the energy of movement.

CHAPTER XII
THE WAVY PATH OF THE AMEBA

In the preceding chapters we discussed the various factors which characterize ameboid movement: the streaming of the endoplasm, the formation of ectoplasm, and the behavior of the surface film. The discussion has involved only momentary cross-sections of the life of an ameba, following the method of investigation in general use for the solving of problems connected with ameboid movement. It has been tacitly assumed that if one could explain ameboid movement at any particular cross-section in time, one understood the whole process of ameboid movement no matter how long it continued, excepting, of course, the action of various kinds of stimuli that produced changes in direction, speed, etc., of streaming. It was not assumed that time was an element in the practical sense in the explanation of locomotion. A few seconds' or a few minutes' comprehensive observation was supposed to furnish sufficient basis for an explanation.

Sometime ago I discovered however that the path of an ameba as it moves over a flat surface free from particles possesses character; it is not an aimless irregular zigzagging here and there, such as has been generally supposed, and in occasional instances asserted, to be the case. On the contrary, the path of an ameba during the course of an hour or two consists of a succession of gentle right and left-hand curves alternating with each other. The general appearance of the path is that of a flattened spiral. Having observed a part of an ameba's path, therefore, one can predict with considerable accuracy in what direction the ameba will continue to move. Thus that scientific bugaboo "Random Movement" is evicted from that strongest of his strongholds, the aimless wanderings of the ameba.

The mechanism producing the sinuosities in the path of the amebas is easily disturbed by external or internal stimulation of various sorts, resembling in this respect the spiral path of a paramecium, which is also easily changed by the presence of various solid and dissolved substances in the culture medium. But the mechanism controlling the direction of the path of an ameba is apparently much more delicate than that in paramecium, for it is only occasionally that a considerable succession of regular sinuosities are described by an ameba in moving over a flat surface. On the other hand, a few fair curves are found in the path of practically every ameba if carefully observed for an hour or more under favorable conditions.

To observe the path an ameba describes in moving over a flat surface, the following conditions must be fulfilled. One must have a small glass dish with a flat bottom, polished preferably, but not necessarily, of the size of a small petri dish, but square so as to fit into a mechanical stage. The dish should be filled with culture fluid free from solid particles. Centrifuging the culture medium, or dialyzing distilled water in the culture medium, will yield a satisfactory medium. It is only by experience that one can pick out an ameba that seems to be in an optimum condition for this purpose, that is, free from strong internal stimuli, such as those from a large mass of food, etc. Just as we speak of "clean-limbed" athletes, meaning thereby a high degree of muscular coördination, so one who has worked with these animals for some time acquires the capacity to pick out "clean-limbed" amebas; though how these differ from others is just as impossible to describe adequately as to tell what a clean-limbed athlete is. But having selected two or three amebas that move in a well coördinated manner and passed them through two or three changes of water free from particles, they are placed in the middle of a dish and allowed to remain for ten or fifteen minutes before observations are begun. A small shade should be placed in front of the dish if very strong light can reach it. It does not matter if diffuse light reaches the dish. A camera lucida with its appurtenances is absolutely essential. In addition to the ordinary precautions the edge of the paper must be laid parallel with the side of the mechanical stage, for a number of sheets of paper will have to be used up in the course of an hour or two and these must be pasted together properly to reconstruct the path. The best magnification shows the ameba two to five cm. long on the paper. Drawings should be made quickly but carefully, beginning and ending with the posterior end of the ameba.

One of the best examples of the sinuous path of an ameba is shown in Figure 33. It is the path of an *Amoeba bigemma* from a natural out-door culture. The observations were made under the conditions outlined above. The temperature, which is an important factor, was unfortunately not recorded, but it was about 28° C.

Practically the whole of the path of this ameba consists of right and left-hand curves which are nearly uniform in length, each wave being about eight to ten times the length of the ameba. Since the drawings were made at intervals of a minute, the waves are therefore from eight to ten minutes long in time, measuring from crest to crest. Some of the waves are flatter than others, for example wave No. 4, but otherwise it is like the others. Wave 7 is a double wave due to a change of direction. Instead of turning to the right at 9:23 the ameba changed its direction and turned to the left. The smoothness with which this turn was made indicates that it originated in the mechanism producing the sinuous course itself, or that it proceeded from a very slight stimulus external to it. At 9:49 the direction of movement was changed again, but just enough to disturb the formation of a smooth wave. The general direction of locomotion was not changed. It may be assumed that this change was produced by a stimulus external to the wave-producing mechanism. The irregularity and shortness of wave 13 was probably due to the same stimulus that disturbed wave 11. Shortly after 9:58 the ameba came within sensing range of a mass of debris which it pushed away and followed, thus causing a change in the direction of movement. Although waves begin to appear again after this, some of them very smooth, they are not typical for they are too short, ranging from a little over three lengths (wave 16) to a little over six lengths (wave 23). It is likely that the disturbance caused by the mass of debris at 9:58 together with the onset of the division crisis produced the succession of atypical waves. An external disturbance that is sufficiently strong to change the direction of locomotion usually persists for the duration of at least one wave length thereafter. It will be noted that the approach of the division crisis did not tend to destroy the action of the wave mechanism, but only slowed down movement and shortened the waves.

FIGURE 33.

Illustrating the path of an *Amoeba bigemma* under controlled conditions, in ordinary diffuse light from a north window. For convenience of reference the waves in the path are numbered from 1 to 23. The figures were drawn with the aid of a camera lucida at intervals of one minute. The path was recorded from 8:58 to 10:26, when fission occurred. After fission, the path of one of the daughter cells was followed for a short time, but the ingestion of a mass of debris destroyed the regularity of the path. The vertical lines at the point where fission occurred indicate that the figures *above* the lines were moved up the length of the lines. The first figure beyond wave 13 was influenced in its movements by a mass of debris lying to its left. Average length of the ameba, 150 microns.

The path of one of the daughter amebas was followed for a short time, in which there is evidence of a wavy path, but it soon came upon a small mass of debris which it ingested and soon thereafter reversed its direction of movement. This behavior made it unprofitable to continue further observation of this ameba. For the gradual change in direction to the left from wave 1 to 6 in the path of the parent ameba, no adequate explanation has suggested itself.

That amebas react to light has been shown by Verworn ('89), Davenport ('97), Harrington and Leaming ('00), Mast ('10) and especially Schaeffer ('17). It appeared desirable therefore to control the rays of light, for it was thought possible that light might be a factor in the formation of the wavy path. Since no method has yet been devised that permits of the observation of the path of the ameba other than a succession of camera lucida outlines, it is impossible to omit light altogether in the experiments. The next best procedure was therefore followed, viz., the alternation of periods of darkness of a few minutes' duration with brief—ten-second—periods of light, to permit the drawing of camera lucida outlines. The dish in which the amebas were observed was placed in a light-tight box and all light excluded except that which passed through "Daylite" glass with an opal surface on both sides between the condenser and the light source. None but parallel beams, passed through a condenser, reached the ameba. The metal parts of the objective were also blackened. The work was done in a dark room.

Figures 34 and 35 show sections of the path of two *Amoeba discoides* under these experimental conditions. The amebas were for the most part in clavate shape, which is the most favorable shape for the formation of smooth waves. In figure 34, from 2:29¼ to 2:42¼ the ameba was in continuous light. A section of a little more than one wave is shown. Although pseudopods were thrown out at considerable distances to the right and left of the path, a smooth, wavy path was nevertheless maintained. At 2:42½ the light was turned off until 2:58½ except for two ten-second flashes at 2:47 and 2:52.

FIGURE 34.

The path of an *Amoeba discoides* under light controlled conditions. At 2:42¼ the light was turned off until 2:52, except for a ten-second flash at 2:47. The smoothness of the wavy path was thus maintained in complete darkness. Length of the ameba, about 400 microns.

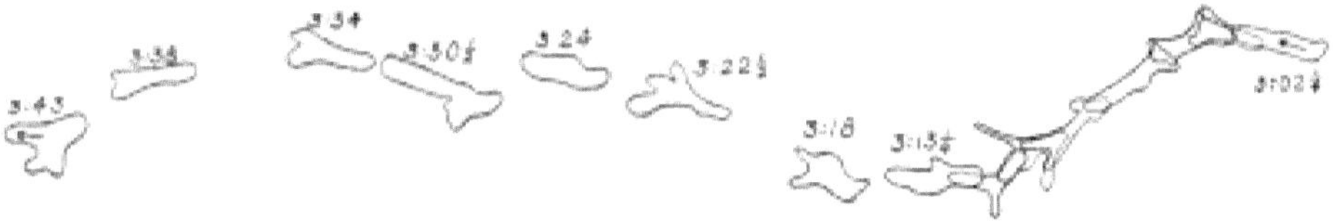

FIGURE 35.

Path of an *Amoeba discoides* showing that continuous light is unnecessary for the maintenance of a wavy path. The ameba moved under light controlled conditions from 3:02¼ to 3:13¼. From then until 3:43 the light was turned off except for 10-second flashes at 3:18, 3:22½, 3:24, and so on. The ameba had probably come to rest for some reason between 3:24 and 3:30½, for an unexpectedly small amount of space was covered in that time. In spite of this disturbance, however, the evidence indicates that light is without causal effect in the wavy path of the ameba. Length of the ameba, 450 microns.

During the first period of darkness the ameba merely kept on in the direction it was going when the light was turned off. But during the second period of darkness the ameba changed its course in such a way as to make a smooth curve. In the third period of darkness the ameba continued on its course completing the wave. It is thus apparent that continuous light is not necessary to the formation of waves nor is it detrimental to their formation. Figure 35 shows essentially the same thing as Figure 34. The light was turned on from 3:30½ to 3:32. During this time the behavior of the ameba was irregular, but whether this was caused by the light or not, cannot be stated. At 3:43 the ameba came into contact with a small particle which changed its course. The slow speed of movement of these two amebas was due to the low temperature (20° C.), the experiments being performed in January. The apparent connection between longer waves and darkness has not yet been investigated.

Figure 36 shows the path of an *Amoeba proteus* under controlled light conditions as above described, but instead of moving over a polished plate glass surface as in the previous experiments, the ameba in this experiment moved over a fine ground-glass surface. It will be observed that for the first twenty minutes the path shows smooth waves, although at 11:53 and 11:55 there was a slight disturbance which was associated with the formation of numerous pseudopods. From 12:07 on, however, the path becomes irregular, the wave-like character being almost obliterated. Associated with this irregularity is the presence of numerous pseudopods. This is a sample of a number of records which indicates that in *proteus* and *discoides* the presence of numerous pseudopods in some way prevents the ameba from moving in a path marked by smooth and conspicuous waves.

FIGURE 36.

Showing how smooth waves in the path of an *Amoeba proteus* in clavate shape become disturbed by the projection of prominent pseudopods. Although there was considerable disturbance due to the formation of pseudopods at 11:53 the conformation of the wave was not changed until the stage preceding the one at 12:07, when the formation of numerous pseudopods resulted in an irregular path. Length of the ameba, about 600 microns.

When a wave in the path for some reason becomes unusually long, there is likely to be a very abrupt and decided change in the direction of movement, which is away from the *convex* side of the wave. Figure 37 is inserted here to illustrate this point. The ameba should have turned to the left at 3:43 to keep the waves of typical size, and at 3:45 a pseudopod was extended in this direction a short distance, but again the curve toward the right persisted. But at 3:48½ the ameba broke up into several pseudopods at right angles with the main axis, and through one of these the ameba moved on with the reestablishment of the wavy path. The tendency to wave formation evidently has to overcome resistance of some sort.

FIGURE 37.

An illustration showing that sudden changes from the expected direction of the wavy path are centrifugal, not centripetal; that is, away from the focus of the wave, not toward it. The tendency to break away from the first smooth wave became apparent at 3:45, as indicated by the extension of pseudopods near the anterior end. In the stage about two minutes later, a number of small pseudopods were thrown out in various directions. At 3:48½ several large pseudopods were thrown out near the anterior end almost at right angles to the main axis, instead of at an angle of about sixty degrees or less, as is the usual case. The same thing occurred at 3:57, except that the angle of the pseudopod was not so large.

FIGURE 38.

Amoeba dubia usually moves with numerous large pseudopods,
but this illustration shows that there is very good reason for con-
cluding that there is a tendency in this ameba to move in wavy
paths. Length of the ameba, 400 microns.

Although amebas in clavate shapes describe the smoothest waves in their
paths, waves may also be detected in the paths of amebas that habitually form
many pseudopods. The path of an *Amoeba dubia* is shown in Figure 38. The ameba
moved on an opal surface under light-controlled conditions. If we had not already
seen how *proteus, discoides,* and especially *bigemma* formed smooth waves in their
paths, we should hardly be able to understand the apparently aimless path of
dubia. But having seen how a regular succession of smooth waves appears under
favorable conditions in the paths of these amebas, there can be little question but
that the staggering path of a *dubia* also is to be interpreted as a succession of waves,
although they are somewhat irregular.

These four species of amebas, *proteus, dubia, discoides* and *bigemma* are the only
species that have been specially investigated as to their paths, and they all show
such paths, as we have seen. The presumption is strong therefore that it is a common characteristic of amebas.

To learn something of the nature of the wave-forming mechanism in the ameba, it is necessary to find some agencies that modify the activity of this mechanism.
That there are such factors is of course evident enough from what has been said

already about wavy paths, and from the appearance of the paths themselves. But the factors which influence the formation of waves in so far as they may be known or reasonably suspected, are internal and therefore difficult to make use of experimentally.

One of the most readily applied stimuli that is known to affect the character of ameboid movement is temperature. In general, the lower the temperature, the slower the movement. This has frequently been observed and recorded. Such behavior is to be expected from a viscous fluid like protoplasm. This may therefore be a purely physical phenomenon. But the lowering of the temperature has also another effect on the movement of amebas: it creates in them a tendency to cross their paths more frequently. Figure 33 is a typical example of the path of an ameba in a high temperature (28° C.). It did not cross its path at all during the hour and a half it was under observation. When the temperature is low (20° C.) the path becomes contracted and the ameba seems unable to get away from the place it happens to be in. Movement of course continues but it is slower, and a large number of loops occur in the path. Figure 39 indicates the general path of an ameba under controlled conditions in a temperature a little lower than room temperature, that is, about 20° C. During the four hours that it was under observation the ameba crossed its path eight times and made a number of very short turns besides. Leaving out of account the loops in the path there are a number of sections which may be interpreted as waves, such as for example the pronounced waves a short distance from the end of the path. All these waves are shorter but much deeper than the waves made in a higher temperature. The loops in the path (all excepting the first, which is a compound loop) represent each a single wave which have become so deep and contracted that they have become transformed into circles. As the temperature decreases, the crests of the waves rise higher and higher, and the bases contract more and more, until the two sides of the waves come together, resulting in the formation of circles (Figure 40). The actual size of the wave also decreases at the same time from about eight times the length until it is only two or three times the length of the ameba. Temperature affects therefore the wave mechanism independently of the mere viscosity of the endoplasm. The speed of movement is not merely slowed down, but the character of the waves themselves is changed.

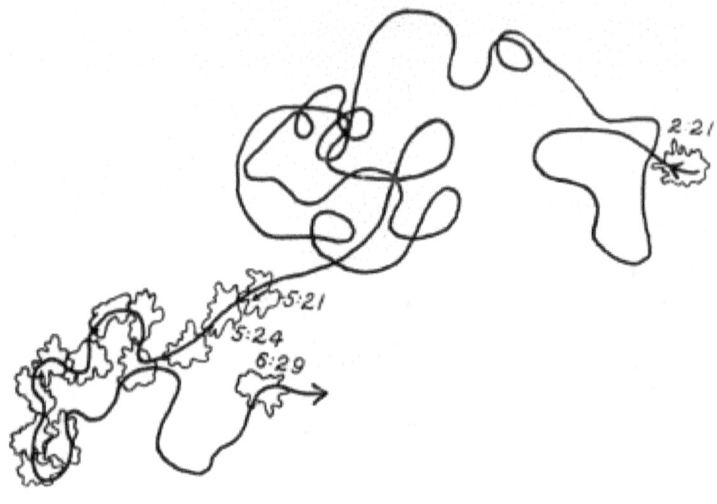

FIGURE 39.

The path of an *Amoeba dubia* in comparatively low temperature (18° C.). The large number of loops and deep waves in the path are due to the low temperature. The experiment was performed under light controlled conditions. Length of the ameba, 350 microns.

Amebas sometimes react to stimuli by moving around the source of the stimulus at a more or less uniform distance through one or more quadrants of a circle, instead of reacting positively, negatively, or indifferently, in a definite manner, to the source of the stimulus (Schaeffer '16, '17). See Figure 41. The explanation that has been given by this investigator is that the encircling is due to a balance between the tendency to move ahead in the original direction ("Functional inertia") and a tendency to react positively. But now that we know that amebas tend to form waves in their paths, the explanation of encircling becomes simpler and perhaps also more convincing.

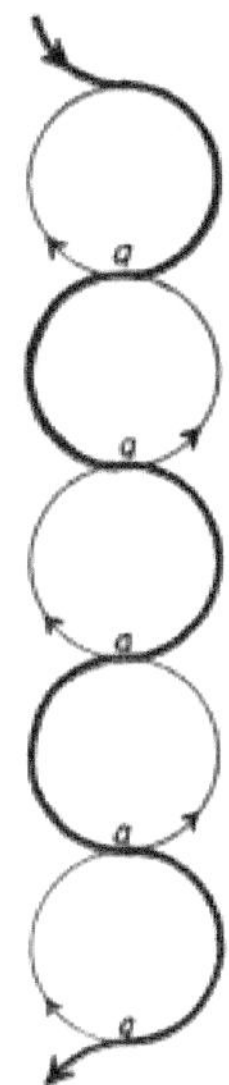

FIGURE 40.

Diagram illustrating how the deepening of the waves in the path of an ameba due to decreased temperature may lead to loops in the path. The heavy line represents the wavy path, and the light lines with the arrows indicate the direction taken when loops are formed. The point in the path where the direction is most easily changed is where one wave grades off into the next, as indicated by the letter *a*.

In the first place, instances of encircling are relatively rare in the reaction of amebas, much rarer than one would expect if it depended merely upon a balance between two tendencies, one to move ahead and the other to move toward the source of the stimulus. Any explanation of this phenomenon has therefore to account for the rarity with which it occurs as well as the operation of the phenomenon itself. This the explanation based upon the position of the source of the stimulus with reference to the configuration of the wavy path can do satisfactorily.

In the experiments with temperature it was found that when the temperature is 20° C. or lower, the waves tend to curl up, to become transformed into circles. That is, the base of one

FIGURE 41.

Showing the phenomenon of encircling, after Schaeffer. The ameba moved around a perpendicular beam of red light. The reaction was neither distinctly positive nor negative.

wave, instead of running into the base of the next wave is reflected backwards to form a circular curve. All the evidence thus indicates that the weakest point is at the base of the wave. A constantly acting stimulus may therefore break the wave here if it cannot break into it elsewhere, and so change the direction of the path. In Figure 42 are shown a few diagramatic waves in the path of an ameba together with several reflected curves at 1, 2 and 3 indicating the points at which the direction is most easily changed as evidenced by the temperature experiments. If a particle within sensing range of the ameba lie at *a*, *b*, or *c*, and stimulate the ameba only slightly but still enough to break up the wave formation, the ameba will take a curved path around the particle as indicated by the dotted lines. But if the same particle lay at any other point with reference to the position of the wave, as at *e*, *f*, or *g*, the ameba would not have changed its course. Briefly, the following conditions must be satisfied to enable the phenomenon of encircling to appear: (1) The particle must lie a little to the side of the ameba's path. (2) It must lie abreast of the point at which the ameba begins to change its direction of movement (i. e., at the base of the wave) when describing waves. (3) It must stimulate the ameba just strong enough positively to break into the wave-forming process. Encircling then is due to a "balance" between a positive stimulus and a tendency to move in a curve. This explanation conforms with all the data at hand and explains also the rarity of the phenomenon, for the chances of encircling occurring on this view are rather less than one-fifth as frequent as if encircling took place whenever a balance between a tendency to react positively and to move straight ahead occurred.

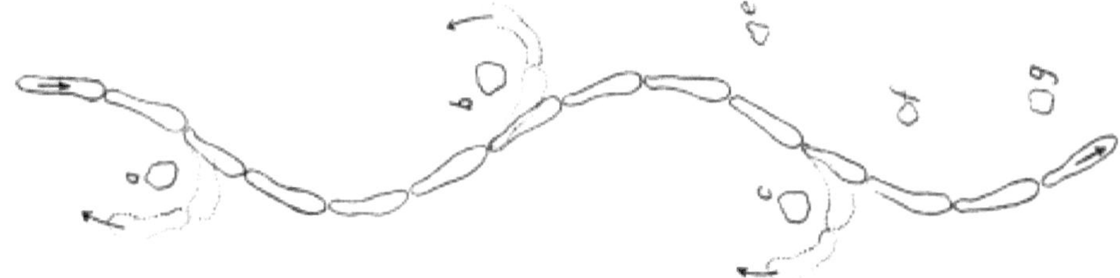

FIGURE 42.

Diagram illustrating the relation of the phenomenon of encircling to the wavy path of the ameba. The weakest point in the path, i. e., where the wave may be broken most easily, is where one wave merges into another, as indicated by the experiments with low temperature, *a*, *b*, *c*. The direction of movement of the ameba is the reverse of what it would have been had there been no stimulus producing encircling. The same stimulus at *e*, *f*, or *g* would not produce encircling because it is more difficult for the ameba to move away from the concave side of the wave.

That the wavy path is broken up by the receipt of a stimulus, that is, by a true sensation, rather than by direct effect of some agency radiating from the particle, is indicated by the fact that stimuli proceeding from various substances, such as keratin, glass, carbon, light beams, etc., have all the same effect.

In attempting to explain the characteristic nature of the path of the ameba, one's attention centers first, perhaps, upon its orderliness; a result undoubtedly of the general impression propagated through hastily written textbooks and general papers, that an ameba's whole life is a direct response to its environment. As the recorded facts of the life of this organism are accumulating, it is coming to be seen that the ameba possesses all the fundamental attributes of animals generally, in addition to many special ones. So that as a matter of fact, if the ameba did not show some character and orderliness in its locomotion, then for the first time should we be especially interested in what would have to be regarded as a very striking and exceptional characteristic.

For it is very well known, and it is generally recognized by everybody, that moving organisms usually move in an orderly manner; it is recognized that organisms tend to move in straight paths excepting where interrupted by the action of some special stimulus. When an organism changes its direction of motion frequently and abruptly, we call it erratic. The mad dashings-about of the hunter-cil-itae *Didinium* and the unceasing gyrations of the whirligig beetle excite one's curiosity because these organisms do not move as other organisms do; they contradict our expectation of movement in a straight line.

But why should organisms generally tend to move in straight paths? This fundamentally important question has received almost no attention, excepting that rapidly moving animals like birds, flying insects, fishes and other rapidly swimming animals of various kinds and rapidly running animals tend to move in straight paths because of the physical inertia of the mass of the organism. It is easier for a rapidly moving organism to move in a straight line than to change its direction of movement frequently and abruptly.

The ameba however is a very slow moving animal, as animals go, for it (*proteus*) moves only about 600 microns per minute. Under the microscope, however, which magnifies speed as well as size, the endoplasmic particles rush along rapidly enough to suggest that even here mere physical inertia might be a determining factor in the path of the ameba, which for considerable segments is often very nearly straight. Such suspicion is not justified, however, for the viscosity of the endoplasm taken in connection with the heterogeneous composition of the ameba, makes it improbable that mere physical inertia can affect the path of the ameba.[5]

It is not even necessary that movement of the endoplasmic stream be interrupted in order that a straight path may be maintained. An ameba may stop movement for a minute or more and then be much more apt to resume movement in the original direction than in any other. This is brought out by the following series of

---

[5] According to Ewart ('03) the viscosity of streaming protoplasm in plant cells lies between $\eta = .04$ and $\eta = .2$. But the velocity of streaming endoplasm in ameba is considerably slower than that in the plant cells which formed the basis for Ewart's calculations. In comparison, we may estimate the viscosity of the endoplasm of ameba as $\eta = .1$ dynes per sq. cm. The velocity of streaming endoplasm, as ascertained by observations on *Amoeba dubia* (in which the endoplasm flows usually rapidly) is $^1/_{880}$ cm. per second.

Now, given a unit mass of endoplasm moving at a given instant with a 1 velocity of $^1/_{880}$ cm. per second against viscosity of $\eta = .1$ dynes per sq. how far will the unit mass travel before coming to rest?

Force = Mass × Acceleration, and Acceleration = Velocity/Time.

η = Viscosity = F = MA = MV/T.

Now if M = 1, η = F = A = V/T.

$T = V/\eta = {}^1/_{880}/_{.1} = {}^1/_{88}.$

The space travelled over in uniformly accelerated motion equals

$S = {}^1/_2 AT^2 = {}^1/_2 \times {}^1/_{10} \times ({}^1/_{88})^2 = {}^1/_{154880} = .00000645$ cm.

If, therefore, the force moving the central stream of endoplasm should suddenly be discontinued, the resistance offered by the viscosity of the enveloping endoplasm would allow it to move only .0000645 mm. before coming to rest. But the ameba as a whole moves more slowly than the central stream of endoplasm, the average rate of movement being about $^1/_{300}$ mm. per second. The effect of the streaming endoplasm on the forward movement of the whole ameba would therefore be correspondingly decreased. Now if the ameba was perfectly homogeneous and perfectly symmetrical, and free from external stimulation, and moved in a perfectly homogeneous liquid on a perfectly plane surface, the excessively small amount of mechanical inertia would then be sufficient, theoretically, to cause the ameba to move in a straight instead of an irregular path. But these conditions are never realized. The ameba is unsymmetrical in form, heterogeneous in composition and always unsymmetrically stimulated; hence it is impossible that the excessively small amount of mechanical inertia can be considered a factor in determining the direction of the ameba's path.

experiments.

Of sixty cases of feeding on various kinds of particles, by as many different amebas, in which the direction of movement before and after a particle was eaten was recorded, thirty-nine moved off in the same direction after eating as before eating. By moving off in the same direction is meant that the ameba did not move more than 22½° to the right or to the left of the direction of movement before feeding. The circle was thus divided into octants, and the expectation of movement in the same direction after eating a particle, if it were a matter of chance, would have been seven and one-half cases instead of thirty-nine.

But it is not only the process of feeding that has to be considered in this connection, for feeding occasionally is affected by a side pseudopod while the main body of the ameba moves on without being visibly affected as to its direction of movement. No such case is included in the figures just given. In each of these sixty cases the endoplasmic streams of locomotion were completely stopped, from about twenty seconds to seventeen minutes. In most cases the endoplasmic stream was also completely disorganized, the ameba assuming a nearly spherical form in which more or less well marked though small cross currents of endoplasm could be detected. The direction of the light was without effect, for the paths extended in every direction with respect to the light both before and after feeding. Further, it has been shown that ordinary diffuse light is without effect on the movements of the ameba (Schaeffer, '17). It may be concluded therefore that the ameba tends to keep on moving in straight paths even if the highly disorganizing act of feeding and the consequent resting period of a few seconds to many minutes supervenes at some point in its path. To what this induction of the original path is due is not clear, thought it is possible that the physical condition of the ectoplasm at the anterior end is different from that elsewhere and that it requires less energy in consequence, or for some other reason, to flow in the original direction. This explanation is based on the observation that it is easier for the ameba to activate the remnants of old pseudopods than to form new ones (Schaeffer, '17).

CHAPTER XIII

THE WAVY PATH OF THE AMEBA AND THE SPIRAL PATHS OF CILIATES AND OTHER ORGANISMS

The most interesting feature of the path of the ameba is of course the waves. The path of an ameba closely resembles the projection of a helical spiral on a plane surface, and this at once calls to mind the spiral swimming of flagellates, ciliates, rotifers, larvae or various groups of animals, swarm spores and zoöspores of various algae and fungi. But before we take up the general subject of spiral movement, it will be worth while to see what other evidence there is beside the wavy path, that indicates that the "spiral urge" is present in the ameba.

It is well known that in a number of the small amebas, especially the soil amebas, there are two trophic stages, an ameboid stage and a free swimming flagellate stage. The change from one stage to the other is a matter of a few minutes only. In the flagellate stage (Figure 43) the amebas resemble a small flagellate like chilomonas, very closely. Their manner of swimming is very similar. And it is especially noteworthy in this respect that they revolve on their long axis and describe a well marked, regular spiral path, just as do the flagellates and ciliates. Unfortunately no records have yet been made of the paths these amebas describe when in the true ameboid stage. Since, therefore, as we shall see later, the slightly unsymmetrical shape of the flagellate stage is not the cause of the spiral path, it is probable that the mechanism controlling the activity of the flagellum can produce orderly locomotion only when the organism follows a spiral path.

Much has been written about the fundamental similarity or identity between flagella and pseudopods. All writers who have expressed themselves on this point incline to think that there is such similarity, that flagella are really very slender and very agile pseudopods. I am not going to record here the evidence for this conclusion, for I have recently had the good fortune to make some very convincing observations on a hitherto undescribed ameba (which for the sake of reference will here be called *flagellipodia*, Figure 44) whose pseudopodia stand about midway between typical flagella and typical pseudopods in their activity.

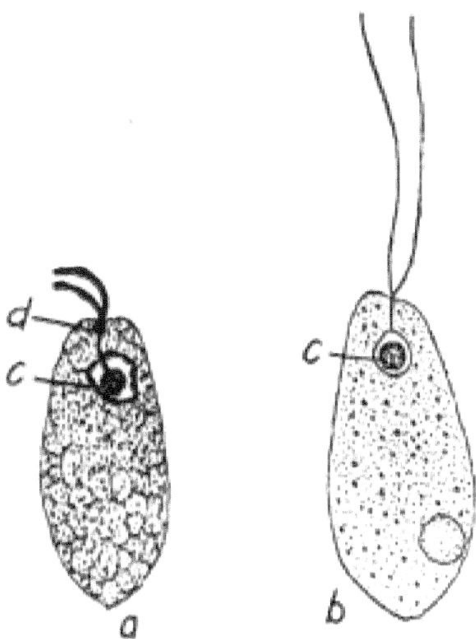

FIGURE 43.

The flagellate stage of a soil ameba, after Wilson. *a*, stained preparation showing the two flagella arising from the blepharoplast, *d*, which is connected with the caryosome, *c*, the central chromatin mass. Much of the chromatin is deposited on the nuclear membrane. *b*, a drawing from a live flagellate showing flagella, nucleus, *c*, and a vacuole.

In its general characteristics it stands near *A. radiosa*, but quite unlike the stiff, static pseudopods which *radiosa* very frequently forms, this ameba has usually five or more slender pseudopods of which one or two or more are in slow flagellate motion. The distal third or half of the pseudopod is in the shape of a corkscrew. The free end of the pseudopod travels around in a circle (anti-clockwise in all instances observed), making one revolution in about three seconds. If this motion were very rapid it would act like a propeller and the ameba would swim through the water. The part of the pseudopod back of the mobile portion is usually also thrown into a spiral of gradually decreasing diameter until the spirality disappears. This portion of the pseudopod is not mobile in the same way that the distal portion is. Sometimes the whole of a pseudopod is thrown into a spiral, all of the turns being of equal size and only slightly motile. More than half of all the pseudopods formed become spiralized at one time or another of their existence, the greater number of these being however relatively immotile. Pseudopods frequently fall into spirals while they are being extended.

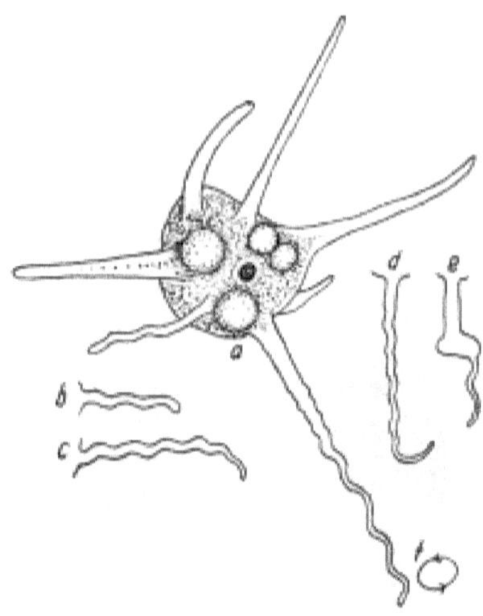

FIGURE 44.

Amoeba flagellipodia. a, showing nucleus, 4 microns in diameter, and four vacuoles. *b,* a pseudopod of three spiral turns which in a few seconds grew into one of six spiral turns, *c. d,* a pseudopod of a number of spiral turns, which a few seconds later took on a shape shown at *e.* The tip of the pseudopod at *f* turned screw-like anti-clockwise, when looking at the tip and at the main body of the ameba. The tip made one complete revolution in about three seconds.

A better transition form between pseudopods and such flagella as are found, for example, in the peranemas, could hardly be imagined. The difference between crawling and swimming would seem to be merely a matter of speed of movement of the pseudopod.[6] But important as such a transition form is for theoretical purposes in understanding the nature of both flagella and pseudopods, it is of special importance for our present purpose because it shows a strong tendency for pseudopods to fall into spirals and to move in spirals. This tendency is found not only in this species of ameba but is observed also occasionally in *radiosa* (Figure 7, p. 30) and in several other species. In these latter species the pseudopods are stiff and not capable of waving about in the water, as are those of *flagellipodia,* whether in the spiral shape or not. In *radiosa* the pseudopods may become spiralized only as a preliminary to withdrawal. It is evident therefore that the spiral urge can express

[6] The gap between the rate of movement of a pseudopod and that of a flagellum is however very wide. Insofar as the *character* of the movement is concerned, pseudopods such as those of *flagellipodia,* probably resemble the flagella of the soil ameba and of flagellates. But the very much greater speed of contraction of a flagellum and the presence of a special organ (blepharoplast) at the base of the flagellum, and their connection with the nucleus, indicates that a special mechanism is necessary to cause the rapid contraction. A flagellum appears to be a pseudopod supplied with something like nerve tissue and a ganglion capable of setting free a rapid succession of impulses.

itself best in a plastic pseudopod.

Taking all these observations together, the tendency of pseudopods to move in a spiral manner, the tendency of the ameba as a whole to move in a spiral path when in the flagellate stage, and the wavy path of amebas which is smoothest when in the clavate stage, all these observations seem to confirm the supposition that the wavy path is in reality a flattened spiral, and that the spiral urge in ameba is a very fundamental factor in the process of locomotion. In other words, there is present in ameba an automatic regulating mechanism controlling the direction of movement so that when free from stimulation a spiral path is followed.

Where can such a mechanism be located? In organisms of fixed form, such as vertebrates, the mechanism controlling and coördinating locomotion is in the central nervous system. Even in some protozoa (*Euplotes*) a motorium has been found whose function apparently is that of coördinating the action of at least some of the motile organs (Sharp, '13, Yocom, '18). But in ameba there is no fixed form. The ameba is continually mixing itself up. No two masses of protoplasm ever occupy the same space relations to each other for more than a moment, excepting perhaps within the nucleus. But the nucleus as a whole is continually changing its position with regard to the rest of the ameba, and almost certainly its position at any given moment in the ameba is the result, not of its own activity, but of the endoplasm and the ectoplasm. A formed nucleus, moreover, is not necessary to concerted movement, for *Protamoeba*, in which no granules of chromatin have been found, and there certainly is no formed nucleus present, moves in a concerted manner, though I am unable to state definitely whether it moves in a wavy path. (I have seen this organism only a few times, and on none of these occasions was I able to make the test). It seems therefore possible that the agency responsible for the movement of amebas in flattened spiral paths can be located at any particular point within the ameba. It seems more likely that this mechanism is a spatial aspect of the intimate colloidal activity occurring in such changes of phase as are associated with the phenomenon of contractility and streaming.

Seeing then that movement in spiral paths is possible in animals not possessed of fixed morphology, it becomes of great interest to see whether the spiral paths of free swimming ciliates, flagellates, etc., are similar to those observed in amebas.

Although the spiral paths of flagellates and swarm spores were first studied by Naegli in 1860, and subsequently discussed by numerous botanists and zoölogists, it was not until Jennings in a number of papers ('98-'04) on the spiral paths of numerous species of one-celled organisms and rotifers, described the essential facts underlying spiral movement, that the significance of this method of locomotion began to be realized. His work marked the beginning of a healthy reaction against the conception of ridiculous simplicity of structure and function which had for several decades been settling upon these organisms. He showed that the spiral path is not a purposeless, senseless reaction on the part of these small organisms, but that it is fraught with meaning, and that it may be regarded as one of the most important of their many activities.

In a paper "On the significance of the spiral swimming of organisms" Jennings

('01) develops the thesis that spiral swimming is an acquired habit, an adaptation which has become fixed in these organisms so that they would not be condemned to swim in circles, which would necessarily follow from their asymmetrical form. The organism, in other words, swims in a spiral in order to be able to swim in a generally straight course. This explanation involves of course the supposition that the unsymmetrical shape of the body was developed first, and then, since this led to circular paths, revolution on the long axis became necessary in order that a straight course might be maintained.

But in the explanation of body form in one of the rotifers he (l. c., p. 376) says: "In some of these primitively bilateral animals this spiral method of swimming has resulted in the production of an unsymmetrical form analogous to that of the infusoria."

It is of course quite possible theoretically, that some of the unsymmetrical structures on an organism that habitually swims in spirals, are the *result* of its spiral swimming, and that other structures which go to make the organism unsymmetrical, are the cause of the spiral swimming. This hypothesis is not an attractive one, however, for, because of the endless variety of asymmetrical differentiation in spiral swimming organisms, it would be impossible to tell for the large majority of organs or organelles whether they were the cause or the effect of spiral swimming.

Before taking up the hypothesis that *all moving organisms are subject to the tendency to move in spiral paths*, a hypothesis which accords with all the known pertinent facts, it may be well to examine the thesis that rotation on the long axis is an adaptation which has been developed to compensate for the effect of an unsymmetrical shape of the body.

It will be noted first that this question cannot be decided by direct observation or experiment. The entire body of real evidence is written in phylogeny, and that is for this purpose a closed book. It is only the interpretations of observations that bear on this problem, and it is these interpretations that it is of interest to examine.

Referring now only to the ciliates, all of which have numerous motile organs, it has been observed by numerous writers that cilia are not confined to one or two methods of contraction, but that there is great latitude in the extent and direction of their activity. This is very well illustrated by a paramecium or a stentor whose ciliary systems enable these animals to execute a great variety of maneuvers depending upon the character of stimulation, the amount of food in the body, etc. (Jennings, '06, Schaeffer, '10). The cilia are under the control of the animal in the same way as the legs and arms of a man are under his control. Now supposing that the bodies of these organisms became unsymmetrical during the phylogenetic history and as a result became unable to continue to swim in a straight path, the pertinent question to ask is: Was it easier for these organisms to learn to revolve on their long axis than to learn to beat their cilia a little harder on the side toward which they swerved? Observation of the forms before us does not afford any evidence that rotation was the easiest solution. Moreover, if it was an acquired habit, is it not strange that it should have been easier to acquire the rotating habit for every single species of the six or seven thousand unicellulars which now obey the spiral urge, as well as the swarm spores and zoöspores, than to change the beat of the cilia in some other way, in at least a few species? This explanation also makes inevitable the assumption that the ancestors of our present unsymmetrical protozoans were symmetrical and swam in straight courses without revolving, a condition of affairs which contrasts strongly with present conditions, for none of the most nearly symmetrical unicellulars and swarm spores now swims without revolving on the long axis. It is therefore exceedingly improbable that spiral swimming is the result of an acquired habit.

Now what evidence is there in support of the hypothesis that the spiral path is a necessary accompaniment of locomotion, except as it may be broken by the effect of stimulation?

As a problem in engineering, it is clear that the shape of the body is not responsible for the spiral course, for almost every conceivable shape is met with in organisms swimming in spiral paths. The frequent spiral turns in the path of stylonychia cannot be the result of the shape of the body, which is almost, if not quite, as well adapted for swimming through the water as is that of a euglena or a fish, but for revolution on its long axis it is not nearly so well adapted. Moreover, some of the euglenas turn the ventral or smaller lip out in the spiral turns, while others turn the dorsal or larger lip out (Mast, '10). Since there is no other asymmetry of shape in these euglenas, it is clear that the shape of the body has nothing to do with causing the spiral path. The immediate cause of spirality must therefore be the work of the motile organ, and not the shape of the body.

Similar observations on paramecium have shown that it is the special action of the cilia of a paramecium that causes it to rotate and not the shape of the body. Again the shape of a *Stentor caeruleus* is subject to very great variation due to varying amounts of food eaten, and to surgical operation, but a spiral path is nevertheless maintained while the body shape undergoes marked changes.

Although all free-swimming unicellular organisms revolve on their long (antero-posterior) axis, an occasional one does not move in spirals. This is observed in the large colonial flagellate *Volvox* occasionally, but not always (Mast, '10). Since it is more frequently seen in the larger individuals, it is probable that the formation of spirals is prevented because of the increased physical inertia of the colony; for the older and larger colonies are much more unsymmetrical than the younger and smaller, owing to the unequal distribution of the reproductive elements. *Spondylomorum* and several other colonial forms describe smaller spirals than smaller solitary organisms. These colonial organisms consisting of from four to twenty thousand cells, each of which may be possessed of cilia, are marvels of locomotory coördination, but it is not at all clear how this coördination is brought about. Since the colonies are symmetrical however, the spirality of the path is clearly due to the special action of the cilia.

Some organisms possess body shapes that seem to be due to the habit of spiral swimming. Jennings ('01) describes a species of rotifer whose body forms a segment of a spiral. When swimming a spiral path is described, "of which its own twisted body forms a part" (p. 376). Elsewhere he has pointed out that the oral groove of a paramecium likewise coincides with its own spiral path. Indications of such correspondence between the axis of a structure and the spiral path the organism possessing it, describes, are numerous among free swimming animals. But such correspondence (with an imaginary spiral path) is also found in organisms that do not swim freely. One of the most interesting of such cases is found in the *Oscillatoriaceae*. In a previous chapter it was seen that many of these organisms are capable of moving about by means of a film of what is probably protoplasm, which moves spirally around the filament. A particle attached to this film describes a spiral path like that of a flagellate or a ciliate. Most of the *Oscillatoriaceae* that are capable of movement, consist of straight filaments; but two of the genera, *Arthrospira* and *Spirulina*, are spirally twisted in such a way that the spiral axis of the filament corresponds approximately to the spiral path of a particle attached to the surface film of an *Oscillatoria* filament, except, of course, in size. (The movement of the surface film of neither *Arthrospira* nor *Spirulina* has been studied).

That the spiral shape of a rotifer, for example, may be caused by swimming in a spiral path might perhaps be regarded as a plausible explanation, but it seems to me that it would be more satisfactory to explain the spiral shape of rotifers and *Arthrospira*, the direction of the oral groove of paramecium and similar structures in other organisms, as due to the same fundamental process that causes the spiral path in locomotion. This explanation is purely mechanistic and avoids the teleological element on which the other explanation ultimately depends.

Most of the asymmetrical shapes of the flagellates, ciliates, rotifers, etc., have originated in phylogeny without regard to swimming in spiral paths, and indeed in spite of it. In spindle-shaped organisms like euglena or paramecium the amount of energy required to revolve on the long axis, as compared with that required for forward movement, is small. But in stylonychia, a dorso-ventrally flattened ciliate, much more energy is required to revolve the animal, proportionally, than is needed for forward movement. It is of course perfectly evident that as a problem in engineering it requires much more energy to revolve a flat plate on its long axis than a spindle-shaped solid, in a dense medium like water. But in spite of all the obstacles to revolution which asymmetry of body form presents, none of them are serious enough to prevent revolution from occurring, unless the keeled rotifer *Euchlanis* (Jennings, '01) presents such a case. Observation would lead one to believe, however, that the compressed body forms of some of the hypotrichans and some of the flagellates such as phacus, have made revolution on the long axis very difficult; but not difficult enough to destroy the tendency to revolve and describe spirals. In short, these organisms spiralize in spite of asymmetry, not because of it.

A simple but decisive experiment by Jennings ('06) showed that the revolution and the forward movement of a paramecium is due to the oblique stroke of the cilia, for the severed posterior portion of a paramecium, which is symmetrical, nevertheless still revolves during progression. The question now arises whether this oblique stroke is analyzable into components in another way than by local stimulation; for example, can one increase or decrease the amount of revolution faster than the amount of progression? Observation of paramecium and euglena in different temperatures answers this question affirmatively. Organisms from the same culture were subjected to two temperatures, the culture temperature of 21° C. and 8° C. At temperatures lower than 8° C. the paramecia quickly precipitated to the bottom of the dish.

In 21° C. paramecia revolve once while swimming 5.5 body lengths.

In 21° C. euglenas revolve once while swimming 4.2 body lengths.

In 8° C. paramecia revolve once while swimming 3.6 body lengths.

In 8° C. euglenas revolve once while swimming ¼ to 2 body lengths.

The effect of decreased temperature is therefore to retard forward movement and to increase proportionally the number of spiral turns, for a revolution of the body on the long axis is the equivalent of one turn in the spiral path. It will be recalled that a similar result was obtained with amebas; in the lower temperature the rate of forward movement was reduced and the tendency to deepen the waves increased. In both these classes of organisms, differences in temperature enable one to separate the forward movement component from the spiral component, in the same way and in general to the same extent.

In clear water of optimum temperature or somewhere near it, paramecia and euglena (*Euglena gracilis*, which does not readily react to light) often swim for long stretches without change of direction. When the temperature is lowered, however, the stretches of straight paths become much shorter. In a temperature of 8° C. changes of direction become very frequent. In paramecium some of these changes are probably due to shock of some sort, judging from mere appearance; but in many cases the change of direction is preceded by a slowing up of forward movement and the swinging of the anterior end in a wide circle one or more times around. Occasionally one observes slow forward movement with wide swinging of the anterior end, for considerable distances. In euglena this condition is more marked than in paramecium; frequently the anterior end spins around with the posterior end as a pivot for several minutes at a time, in low temperatures.

These observations are strikingly analogous to the circles formed in the paths of amebas in low temperatures, and geometrically they bear the same relation to the spiral paths of ciliates and flagellates as the circles do to the wavy path of the ameba.

Besides the effect of temperature on paramecium and euglena, effects which are continuous and automatic, it is of course well known that the spiral path may be readily broken into by appropriate stimulation of the sense organs. The automatic locomotory mechanism is then for the time being controlled with reference to the character of the stimulus and the experience of the organism. But as soon as the effect of the stimulus has disappeared, the automatic mechanism again controls locomotion.

Sense organs of orientation, including organs of equilibration, break in upon the spiral mechanism controlling direction of movement, and eliminate its effect. It thus happens that no animals with image-forming eyes or equilibrating organs move in spirals in three-dimensional space when these organs are functional. Conversely, animals without image-forming eyes or equilibrating organs move in spiral paths. In addition to the ciliates, flagellates, protophyta, swarm spores and zoö-spores of algae and fungi, Oscillatoriaceae and rotifers, may also be mentioned the larvae of many worms, echinoderms and molluscs. All these are within the grip of the spiral urge. The grip is indeed slight, as we have seen, but in the absence of stimulation it is none the less absolute.

The movements of none of the animals in the higher groups have been studied in any detail. Excepting the movements of some of the ciliates, flagellates, amebas, rotifers, a few scattered protophyta and swarm spores our knowledge of the movements of spiral swimming organisms is of the most casual and fragmentary sort. Nothing beyond the mere fact that these organisms describe some kind of a spiral swimming, is known.

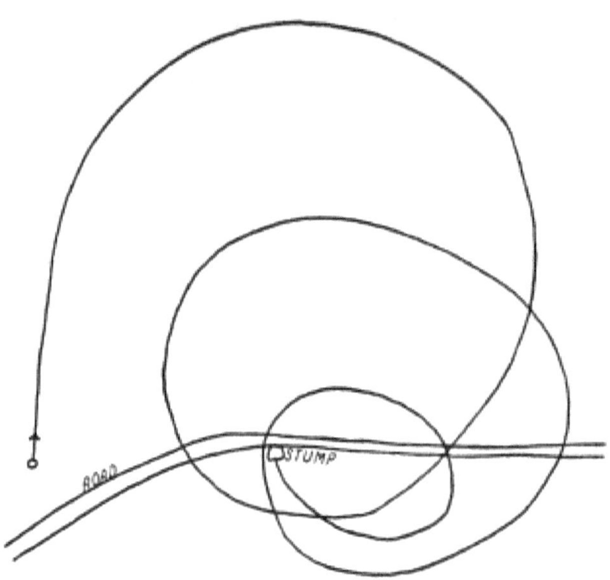

FIGURE 45.

Showing the path walked by a normal right-handed man (J. N.), blindfolded and counting his paces. The whole path was 546 paces long. The command given was to walk in the direction of the arrow until halted. The field was slightly rolling. The stump made necessary a termination of the experiment.

That a spiralizing mechanism is probably also present in organisms with highly developed equilibrating and orienting senses would be the logical expectation from what has been said regarding the presence of such a mechanism in the lower forms of life; but the effect of such a mechanism would naturally be suppressed when the orienting senses are functioning. To test this point, man was selected for experiment. With eyes blindfolded and ears plugged (this latter precaution was subsequently found to be unnecessary) so as to render the orienting senses ineffective, a normal man was directed to walk straight ahead over a large field towards an object he had just looked at. Although a number of experiments were made with several individuals, *none of them was able to walk a straight path. All of them walked true spirals or series of circles with remarkably smooth curves* (Figures 45, 46). The spirals were right and left handed in the same individual, and sometimes in the same experiment. In these experiments the subject was totally unconscious of the direction in which he was walking. No effort of consciousness seemed capable of changing the *degree of curvature* of the spiral or circle and keep it smooth, though one could of course at any time break into the spiral or circle and walk off in another direction. (The writer himself walked in several experiments.) If one has one's mind *strongly* on the direction of walking, thinking of each step, the curve of the path shows small "wabbles"; but if one recites something or counts his paces, the curves are quite smooth.

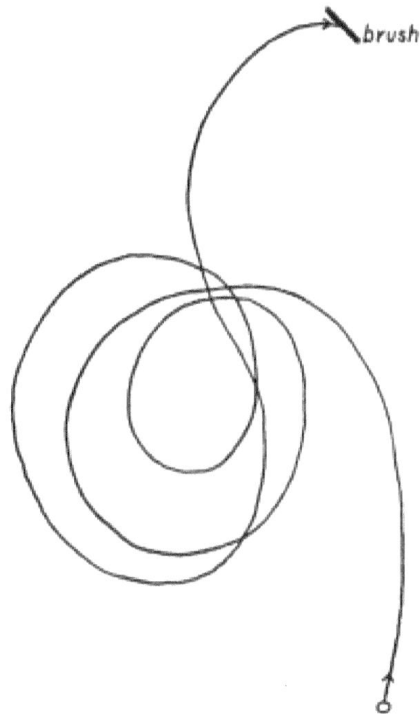

FIGURE 46.

Illustrating a path walked by a normal right-handed man (J. D.), blindfolded and counting his paces. The path was 560 paces long and was walked over the same field as the path illustrated in figure 45. The path had to be terminated because of a clump of brush.

Considerable unevenness of the ground has no effect on the curvature of the spiral. Structural differences in the legs are also without effect, for a person with one artificial leg walks quite as smooth a spiral as one with two normal limbs.[7]

[7] It should be added here that since this paragraph was written I have been very fortunate to secure numerous records of paths swam by blindfolded swimmers, which

From these experiments on man, it follows that there is a "centre" in the central nervous system which automatically coördinates and controls movement during locomotion and, particularly from the point of view of this discussion, the direction of locomotion when the orienting senses are not functioning. This center must be very deep seated and automatic, and in so far as its influencing the direction of locomotion is concerned, it is of no discoverable use to man. It may be presumed to have existed before the present orienting senses originated in man, for there is very good evidence that horses and perhaps dogs, too, possess this mechanism. For these animals, like man, tend to walk in circles when lost, a peculiarity of behavior undoubtedly due to the activity of this mechanism and not to stronger right or left legs, etc., as has often been suggested (e. g., Thompson, '17, p. 498). According to the accounts of experienced hunters, rabbits also run in circles when hard pressed by hounds, which may possibly be due to the suppression of the functioning of the orienting senses by fear, thus allowing the automatic directing mechanism to operate.

The facts are therefore that all organisms without orienting senses or equilibrating organs, or animals possessing such organs which are rendered ineffective by some means, will not move in straight paths nor in any kind of irregular path, but *in orderly paths*, so that a given segment of the path serves as a basis for predicting the further direction of the path. And the degree of accuracy to which such prediction may attain is proportional to the extent to which the activity of the automatic regulating mechanism may be kept free from outside interference. The organisms of which this holds true include, as far as known, all the free-swimming unicellulars, swarm spores of algae and fungi, uni-and multinucleate zoöspores, rotifers, a large number of worms and worm larvae of all classes (excepting the nematodes) and the larvae of many molluscs, echinoderms and copepods as well as some adult copepods. Organisms restricted to two dimensions of space in their movements, in which orderly paths have been recorded, are ameba and man and perhaps we may include the horse and the dog. This is indeed only a small number of organisms compared with all that can move; but there are representatives in the list of all the large groups excepting the higher plants, and without doubt observation will greatly extend the list, for there are mentioned here only such organisms whose movements have been definitely recorded or personally observed. As far as now known, no organism lacking orienting organs moves in a straight line. Many spermatozoa with flagellate tails seem, however, to do so, but no careful studies of their paths have yet been made.[8]

strikingly resemble those of persons walking blindfolded as described above. Most of the common swimming strokes were employed in these observations and occasionally several strokes were employed in a single experiment. In a few cases the spiral path was made up of over twenty turns, and in one case of over fifty turns. A fuller discussion of these results does not seem pertinent here, and must be deferred to a later date.

[8] Since this was written I have been able to examine the movement of live sperm cells in a number of representative animals, including the jellyfish *Aurelia*; the molluscs *Ostrea, Solemya, Pandora*; the arthropods *Limulus* and *Anisolabia,* and the vertebrates frog, turtle, snake, cat, dog and man, with the result that all these spermatozoa revolve on their long axes and swim in spiral paths resembling those of flagellates. Owing to their minute size their movements are made out only with great difficulty, but so far as could be deter-

The orderliness of the paths of these organisms when moving under such conditions as described above, is itself orderly; that is, the path of all these organisms is a spiral of one kind or another: (1) a helical spiral, as in the free-swimming unicellulars; (2) a true spiral in one plane, as in man; (3) a helical spiral projected on a plane surface, as in ameba.

These facts point inevitably to the hypothesis that the movements of these and all other moving organisms are controlled by an automatic regulating mechanism, which is of essentially similar nature in all organisms, as is indicated by the tendency to spiralize the path. This mechanism, being automatic, absolutely controls the direction of the path so long as outside interferences permit; but when sensory stimulation occurs, or when changes in temperature, etc. occur, the mechanism is no longer able to operate automatically or smoothly. The direction of the path then depends upon the nature and direction from which stimulation was received, and upon the degree and direction of change of temperature, etc.

The importance of this conception of movement lies in the fact that it enables us to look at a large mass of otherwise unrelated data from a single point of view. Secondly, it permits of a mathematical treatment of the whole subject of movement in organisms. And third, it replaces a teleological explanation of spiral movement in unicellulars, swarm spores, rotifers, etc., with a purely mechanistic explanation.

---

mined all the sperms of any one species turn on their axes in the same way, that is, either right-handed or left-handed. Recently there has also come to my notice the very informing paper of W. D. Hoyt, 1910, in the *Botanical Gazette*, in which it is stated that fern sperms of various species swim in spiral paths.

CHAPTER XIV

CONCLUSIONS

One of the most important results of recent work on the movements of ameba and of streaming endoplasm in plant cells is the rapidly growing conviction that the streaming of protoplasm, wherever it is found, is due to the same fundamental cause. The value of this conception lies in the greatly widened front that is presented for attacking the general problem of streaming. The many special aspects of streaming, which in the past have been thought to be essential or fundamental processes, may thus be placed against each other, following what is known as the comparative method, and the main problem will thus be freed of much that is not strictly relevant. In this way we come at once to the heart of the problem.

One of these special aspects of streaming in amebas is the formation of ectoplasm. For ectoplasm formation is not essential to streaming. But it is almost certainly essential to locomotion, for locomotion has not been observed in amebas where ectoplasm was not formed. But, on the other hand, ectoplasm, as known in the amebas, is not formed without streaming, although observations indicate that ectoplasm may suddenly and temporarily pass into the gel state (*Vallisneria*). Streaming is therefore the fundamental process in ameboid locomotion.

The surface layer of the ameba is physiologically distinct from the ectoplasm, although it differs from ectoplasm chiefly, if not wholly, by virtue of its position only. That is, the surface layer is a true surface tension film. There are no observations recorded which actually show that the surface film of the ameba is a semi-permeable or plasma membrane; but, on the other hand, there are no observations which speak against such a supposition. On theoretical grounds the conclusion is justifiable that the surface film as demonstrated by the movements of attached particles is the plasma membrane.

The similarity of the movements of the surface film in ameba with the movements of the superficial films of *Oscillatoria* filaments, diatoms, crawling euglenas, and probably also Gregarinidas, indicates that the superficial films of all these organisms, including amebas, are all activated by surface tension changes. Thus instead of postulating several methods of locomotion which are fundamentally different from each other, for these respective organisms (excepting the ameba), one explanation serves the purpose; and it has the further merit of agreeing more nearly with observation than the various other theories proposed.

From the point of view of ameboid movement, the discovery of the surface film and its activities narrows down the problem very considerably. It does not help *directly* perhaps, in the solution of ameboid movement, but it shows clearly that the region where ectoplasm is most rapidly formed (at the anterior ends of pseudopods) is also the region where the superficial tension is increased. This therefore gives us somewhat of an insight into what must take place during the transformation of endoplasm into ectoplasm.

Although the wavy path of the ameba does not at present relate itself to any other process in the ameba, it is bound to be of the greatest significance in investigating the intimate nature of protoplasm while in movement. In so far as the wavy path concerns the ameba, it effectively disproves the presence of that scientific monstrosity, random movement. The path of the ameba is orderly.

The wavy path of the ameba represents a projection on a plane surface of a helical spiral. The path of the ameba is thus geometrically related to the spiral paths of free-swimming organisms such as ciliates, flagellates, rotifers, swarm spores, worm larvae, etc. But the paths are more closely related than merely geometrically. The effects produced by temperature on amebas and ciliates and flagellates indicate a relationship between the physical processes underlying the control of the direction of the paths traveled over in free movement. No causal distinction can yet be made between rotation on the long axis and the spiral swinging.

The spiral path is not an acquired habit. It is not a habit that has been developed to overcome asymmetry of body shape, for some spirally swimming organisms are not asymmetrical enough to make swimming in spirals necessary. It is also unlikely that so many thousands of species of animals and plants of widely different groups would hit upon the same complex habit to solve widely different problems; for it is not equally important that all animals should swim in straight paths. It also necessitates supposing that the ancestors of our present ciliates, flagellates, rotifers, swarm spores, zoöspores, etc., were symmetrical and swam without revolving on the long axis and without forming spirals. Such an assumption is too formidable and makes the explanation top-heavy.

Spiral swimming is supposed to be due to an automatic regulating mechanism which is present in all moving organisms. It is held to be a spatial aspect of the physical processes originating and controlling movement. The property of moving automatically in an orderly path is inherent in organisms in the same way, e.g., as the property of growth is. A spiral path will be followed whenever an organism is free to move, that is, when not disturbed by sensory stimulation. Slight stimulation is often without effect. The justification of supposing that probably all moving organisms are within the grip of the spiral urge is found in the fact that the amebas, ciliates, flagellates, swarm spores, zoöspores, Oscillatoria, diatoms, rotifers, larvae of worms, molluscs and echinoderms, oligochaets, copepods, as well as man, all move in regular smooth spirals of one kind or another when free from strong stimulation, and that no organism that is free to move as these are, moves in a straight or irregular path.

The observations indicate that the same type of mechanism that controls the direction of the path of an organism also unifies and coördinates the streaming of the protoplasm of the ameba, the action of the cilia of the paramecium, or the contraction of the muscles of man, as the case may be. Why the automatic mechanism controlling the direction of movement should produce a helical spiral in paramecium, a wavy path or flattened spiral in ameba, and a series of spirals in man, is not yet subject to profitable discussion, except of course to point out that paramecium is not restricted to two dimensions of space as is ameba and man. In the nature of the case there can be no question but that the mechanism is one that attaches to the fundamental structure of protoplasm rather than to the gross morphology. As a mathematical question, however, the circles occurring in the path of an ameba in low temperature may serve to connect up the flattened spiral path of the ameba under optimum conditions with the circular path often observed in man.

The movement of the ameba thus becomes related to crawling euglenas, Oscillatoria filaments, diatoms, and perhaps Gregarinidas, because of the movements of its surface layer; to leucocytes, streaming protoplasm in the higher plant cells, etc., because of its streaming endoplasm; and to the locomotory movements of all organisms because of the wavy character of its path, which betrays the activity of an automatic regulating mechanism, a type of which is held to be present in every moving organism.

BIBLIOGRAPHY

Allee, W. C. 1916. Chemical control of rheotaxis in *Asellus*. Jour. Exp. Zoöl., Vol. 21, pp. 163-198.

Amici, 1818. Mem. della Soc. Ital. delle Scienze in Modena, Vol. 18, p. 182.

Arey, L. B. 1915. The orientation of *Amphioxus* during locomotion. Journ. Exp. Zoöl., Vol. 19, pp. 37-44.

Awerinzew, S. 1903. Beiträge zur Kenntniss der marinen Rhizopoden. Mitteil. d. zoöl. Stat. Neapel, Vol. 16.

Awerinzew, S. 1904. Ueber die Teilung bei *Amoeba proteus* Pall. Zoöl. Anz., Vol. 27, pp. 399-400.

Awerinzew, S. 1906. Rhizopoda des Süsswassers. Trav. Soc. Natu. St. Petersbourg, Vol. 36.

Awerinzew, S. 1907. Beiträge zur Structur des Protoplasma und des Kerns von *Amoeba proteus* Pall. Zoöl. Anz., Vol. 32, pp. 45-51.

Bancroft, F. W. 1913. Heliotropism, differential sensibility, and galvanotropism in *Euglena*. Journ. Exp. Zoöl., Vol. 15, pp. 383-428.

Bancroft, W. D. 1914. The theory of colloid chemistry. Jour. Phys. Chem., Vol. 18, pp. 549-558.

Bancroft, W. D. 1913. The theory of emulsification. Jour. Phys. Chem., Vol. 17, pp. 501-520.

Baranetzky, J. 1876. Influence de la lumière sur les plasmodia des Myxomycètes. Mem. Soc. Sc. Nat. Cherbourg, Vol. 19, pp. 321-360.

Barrat, J. O. W. 1905. Der Einfluss der Koncentration auf die Chemotaxis. Zeit. all Physiol., Vol. 5, pp. 73-94.

Baunacke, W. 1913. Studien zur Frage nach der Statocystenfunktion. Biol. Centr., Vol. 33, pp. 427-452.

Bechhold, H. 1905. Structurbildung in Gallerten. Zeit. physik. Chem., Vol. 52, pp. 185-199.

Bechhold, H. 1912. Die Kolloide in der Biologie und Medizin. Dresden und Leipzig, 480 pp.

Becquerel, 1838. Ann. d. sci. nat., Vol. 9, p. 78.

Beer, Th. 1898. Vergleichend-physiologische Studien zur Statocystenfunktion. Arch. ges. Physiol., Vol. 73, pp. 1-41.

Bemmelen, J. M. 1898. Die Absorption. Zeit. anorg. Chem., Vol. 18, pp. 14-37.

Bernstein, J. 1900. Chemotropische Bewegungen eines Quecksilbertropfens. Arch. ges. Physiol., Vol. 80, pp. 628-637.

Bernstein, J. 1901. Die Energie des Muskels als Oberflächenenergie. Arch. ges. Physiol., Vol. 85, pp. 271-312.

Bernstein, J. 1901. Die Kräfte der Bewegung in der lebenden Substanz. Naturwiss. Rundschau, pp. 1413-1415; 429-432; 441-443.

Berthold, G. 1886. Studien über Protoplasmamechanik. Leipzig.

Blohmann, F. 1894. Kleine Mitteilungen über Protozoen. Biol. Centralbl., Vol. 14, pp. 82-91.

Bohn, G. 1909. La naissance de l'intelligence. Paris.

Bohn, G. 1909. Les tropismes. Rapport VIme Congr. Internat. Psychol. Geneve, pp. 15.

Bohn, G. 1911. Le nouvelle psychologie animale. Paris. pp. 200.

Braun, A. 1852. Über die Richtungsverhältnisse der Saftströme in den Zellen der Characeen. Berlin.

Brücke, E. 1864. Untersuchungen über das Protoplasma und die Contractilität. Sitzungsb. d. Wien. Akad., Vol. 56, pp. 36.

v. Buddenbrock, W. 1911. Untersuchungen über die Schwimmbewegungen und die Statocysten der Gattung *Pecten*. Sitzungsb. Heidelberger Akad. Wiss., math.-naturw., pp. 24.

v. Buddenbrock, W. 1912. Über die Funktion der Statocysten von *Branchiomma vesiculosum*. Verhandl. naturhist.-med. Vereines, Heidelberg, 1913. Vol. 12, pp. 256-261.

Buller, A. H. R. 1900. Contributions to the knowledge of the physiology of the spermatozoa of ferns. Ann. Bot., Vol. 14, pp. 543-582.

Bütschli, O. 1880-1882. Protozoa. Bronn's Thierreich. Leipzig.

Bütschli, O. 1892. Untersuchungen über mikroscopische Schaüme und das Protoplasma. Leipzig.

Bütschli, O. 1892. Bewegungen der Diatomeen. Vhdl. Naturh.-med. Vereins Heidelberg, N. F., Vol. 4, p. 580.

Calkins, G. N. 1904. Evidences of a sexual cycle in *Amoeba proteus*. Archiv. f. Protistenk., Vol. 5, pp. 1-16.

Calkins, G. N. 1912. Genera and species of ameba. Trans. 15th Internat. Cong. Hyg. and Demography.

Carter, H. J. 1856. Notes on the fresh water infusoria of the Island of Bombay. Ann. and Mag. of Nat. Hist., Vol. 18, pp. 115, 221.

Chambers, R., Jr. 1915. Microdissection studies on the physical properties of protoplasm. Lancet-Clinic, pp. 1-8.

Chambers, R., Jr. 1917. Microdissection studies. The visible structure of cell protoplasm and death changes. Amer. Jour. Physiol., Vol. 43, pp. 1-13.

Child, C. M. 1915. Individuality in organisms. Univ. of Chicago Press.

Clowes, G. H. A. 1916. Protoplasmic equilibrium. Jour. Phys. Chem., Vol. 20, pp. 407-451.

Clowes, G. H. A. 1916. Antagonistic electrolyte effects in physical and biological systems. Science, Vol. 43, pp. 750-757.

Coehn, A. and Barrat. 1905. Über Galvanotaxis vom Standpunkte der physikalischen Chemie. Zeit. allgem. Physiol., Vol. 5, pp. 1-19.

Cornetz, V. 1912. Über den Gebrauch des Ausdruckes "tropisch" und über den Character der Richtungskraft bei Ameisen. Archiv. ges. Physiol., Vol. 147, pp. 215-233.

Corti, 1774. Osservazioni microscopiche sulla Tremella e sulla circolazione del fluido in una pianta acquaiola. pp. 127. Lucca.

Czapek, F. 1898. Weitere Beiträge zur Kenntniss der geotropischen Reizbewegungen. Jahr. Wiss Bot., Vol. 32, pp. 175-308.

Dale, H. H. 1901. Galvanotaxis and chemotaxis of ciliate infusoria. Journ. Physiol., Vol. 34, pp. 291-361.

Dale, H. H. 1912. The anaphylactic reaction of plain muscle in the guinea pig. Jour. Pharm. Exper. Therap., Vol. 4, pp. 167-223.

Davenport, C. B. 1897. Experimental morphology. New York.

Davenport, C. B., and Cannon, W. B. 1897. On the determination of the direction and rate of movement of organisms by light. Journ. Physiol., Vol. 21, pp. 22-32.

Davenport, C. B., and Lewis, F. T. 1899. Phototaxis of *Daphnia*. Science, Vol. 9, p. 368.

Davenport, C. B., and Perkins, H. 1897. A contribution to the study of geotaxis in the higher animals. Jour. Physiol., Vol. 22, pp. 99-110.

Delage, Y. 1887. Sur une fonction nouvelle des otocystes comme organes d'orientation locomotrice. Arch. zoöl. exper. et gener., Vol. 4.

Dellinger; O. P. 1906. Locomotion of amoebae and allied forms. Jour. Exp. Zoöl., Vol. 13, pp. 337-358.

Dellinger, O. P. 1909. The cilium as a key to the structure of contractile protoplasm. Jour. Morphol., Vol. 20, 170-209.

Dobell, C. C. 1914. Cytological studies of three species of *Amoeba—A. lacertae* Hartmann, *A. glebae* n. sp. and *A. fluvialis* n. sp. Arch. f. Protistenk., Vol. 34, pp. 139-189.

Doflein, F. 1911. Lehrbuch der Protozoenkunde. Jena.

Englemann, T. W. 1879. Über Reizung contractilen Protoplasmas durch plötzliche Beleuchtung. Arch. ges. Physiol., Vol. 19, pp. 1-7.

Ewart, A. J. 1903. Protoplasmic streaming in plants. Oxford.

Flemming, W. 1882. Zellsubstanz, Kern und Ze11theilung. Leipzig.

Flemming, W. 1896. Zelle. Anat. Hefte. Ergebn. Vol. 5, pp. 233-328.

Freundlich, H. 1909. Kapillarchemie. Leipzig.

Gaidukov, N. 1910. Dunkelfeld Beleuchtung und Ultramicroscopie in der Biologie und Medezin. Jena.

Gibbs, J. W. 1878. Equilibrium of heterogeneous substances. Trans. Conn. Acad. Arts and Sciences, Vol. 3, pp. 380-400.

Gibbs, D. and Dellinger, O. P. 1908. The daily life of *Amoeba proteus*. Amer. Jour. Psychol., Vol. 19, pp. 230-241.

Gläser, H. 1912. Untersuchungen über die Teilung einiger Amöben. Arch. f. Protestenk., Vol. 25, pp. 27-152.

Graham, T. 1861. Liquid diffusion applied to analysis. Phil. Trans., Vol. 151, pp. 183-224; 552-600.

Greef, R. 1891. Über den Organismus der Amöben. Biol. Centrl., Vol. II, pp. 599-639.

Greely, A. W. 1904. Experiments on the physical structure of the protoplasm of paramecium and its relation to the reactions of the organism to thermal, chemical and electrical stimuli. Biol. Bull., Vol. 7, pp. 3-32.

Grosse-Allermann, W. 1909. Studien über *Amoeba terricola* Greef. Arch. f. Protistenk., Vol. 17, pp. 203-257.

Gruber, K. 1911. Über eigenartige Körperformen von *Amoeba proteus*. Arch. f. Protistenk., Vol. 23, pp. 252-262.

Gruber, K. 1912. Biologische und experimentelle Untersuchungen an *Amoeba proteus*. Arch. f. Protistenk., Vol. 25, pp. 316-376.

Hanstein, 1880. Protoplasma. Heidelberg.

Harrington, N. R., and Leaming, E. 1900. The reaction of ameba to lights of different colors. Amer. Jour. Physiol., Vol. 3, pp. 9-18.

Hartmann, M. 1914. Bemerkungen über *Amoeba lacertae* Hartmann, eine Antwort an Clifford Dobell. Arch. f. Protistenk., Vol. 34, pp. 336-339.

Hegner, R. W. 1918. Variation and heredity during the vegetative reproduction of *Arcella dentata*. Proc. Nat. Acad. Sci., Vol. 4, pp. 283-288.

Heidenhain, R. 1863. Stud. d. physiol. Inst. Breslau, Vol. 2, p. 60.

Heidenhain, M. 1911. Plasma und Zelle. Bardeleben, Handb. der Anat. d. Menschen. Jena.

Hertwig, R. 1902. Die Protozoen und die Ze11theorie. Arch. f. Protistenk., Vol. 1.

Hirschfeld, L. 1909. Ein Versuch einige Lebenserscheinungen der Amoeben physikalisch-chemisch zuerklären. Zeit. f. all. Physiol., Vol. 9, pp. 529.

Höber, R. 1911. Physikalische Chemie der Zelle und der Gewebe. Leipzig.

Hofer, B. 1890. Experimentelle Untersuchungen über den Einfluss des Kerns auf das Protoplasma. Jen. Zeit., Vol. 24, p. 105.

Hofmeister, W. 1867. Pflanzenzelle.

Holmes, S. J. 1905. The selection of random movements as a factor in phototaxis. Jour. Comp. Neur. and Psychol., Vol. 15, pp. 98-112.

Hörmann, G. 1898. Studien über die Protoplasmaströmung der Characeen. Jena.

Howell, W. H. 1916. Structure of the fibrin gel and theories of gel formation. Amer. Jour. Physiol., Vol. 40, pp. 526-545.

Hyman, L. H. 1917. Metabolic gradients in ameba and their relation to the mechanism of ameboid movement. Jour. Exp. Zoöl., Vol. 24, pp. 55-99.

Hyman, L. H. 1918. Bioelectric phenomena. Science, Vol. 48, p. 518.

Jennings, H. S. 1899. Studies on reactions to stimuli in unicellular organisms. The mechanism of the motor reactions of paramecium. Amer. Jour. Physiol., Vol. 2, pp. 311-341.

Jennings, H. S. 1901. On the significance of the spiral swimming in organisms. Amer. Nat., Vol. 35, 369-378.

Jennings, H. S. 1904. Contributions to the study of the behavior of the lower organisms. Washington.

Jennings, H. S. 1906. Behavior of the lower organisms. New York.

Jensen, P. 1901. Untersuchungen über protoplasmamechanik. Arch. f. d. ges. Physiol., Vol. 87, pp. 361.

Jensen, P. 1902. Die Protoplasmabewegung. Ergeb. d. Physiol., p. 42.

Jensen, P. 1905. Zur Theorie der Protoplasmabewegung. Anat. Hefte, Vol. 27, pp. 829-858.

Kite, G. L. 1913. Studies on the physical properties of protoplasm. Amer. Jour. Physiol., Vol. 32, pp. 146-165.

Klebs, G. 1885. Biol. Centralbl. Vol. 5, p. 353.

Kühne, W. 1864. Untersuchungen über das Protoplasma und die Kontractilität. Leipzig.

Küster, E. 1910. Über Veränderungen der Plasmaoberfläche bei Plasmolyse. Zeit. f. Botan., pp. 689-717.

Kusano, S. 1909. Studies on the chemotactic and other related reactions of the swarm spores of myxomycetes. Jour. Coll. Agri., Imp. Univ. Tokyo, Vol. 2.

Leduc, S. 1912. Le biologie synthetique. Paris.

Lee, F. S. 1894-1895. A study of the sense of equilibrium in fishes. Jour. Physiol., Vol. 17, pp. 192-210.

Lehmann, O. 1910. Flüssige Kristalle. Myelenformen und Muskelkraft. München, p. 43.

Leidy, J. 1879. The freshwater rhizopods of North America. Washington.

Lewis, W. C. M. 1910. Die Absorption in ihrer Beziehung zur Gibbschen Theorie. Zeit. Chemie, Vol. 70, pp. 129.

Lillie, R. S. 1906. The relation between contractility and coagulation of the colloids in the ctenophore swimming plate. Amer. Jour. Physiol., Vol. 16, pp. 117-129.

Lillie, R. S. 1908. The relation of ions to contractile processes. Amer. Jour. Physiol., Vol. 22, pp. 75-90.

Loeb, J. 1900. Comparative physiology of the brain and comparative psychology. New York.

Loeb, J. 1906. The dynamics of living matter. New York.

Loeb, J. 1918. Forced movements, tropisms and animal conduct. Philadelphia.

McClendon, J. F. 1909. Protozoan studies. Jour. Exp. Zoöl., Vol. 6, pp. 265-283.

McClendon, J. F. 1911. Ein Versuch amoeboide Bewegung als Folgeerscheinung wechselnden elektrischen Polarisationszustandes der Plasmahaut zu erklären. Arch. f. d. ges. Physiol., Vol. 140, pp. 271-280.

Mach, E. 1875. Grundlinien der Lehre von der Bewegungsempfindungen. Leipzig.

Mast, S. O. 1910. Light and the behavior of organisms.

Mast, S. O., and Root, F. M. 1916. Observations on ameba feeding on rotifers, nematodes and ciliates and their bearing on the surface tension theory. Jour. Exp. Zoöl., Vol. 21, pp. 33-51.

Mathews, A. P. 1916. Physiological chemistry. Sec. Ed. New York.

Maxwell, S. S. 1910. Experiments on the functions on the internal ear. Univ. Cal. Publ. Physiol., Vol. 4, pp. 1-4.

Michaelis, L. 1909. Dynamik der Oberflächen. Dresden.

Moore, A. R. 1916. The mechanism of orientation in *Gonium*. Jour. Exp. Zoöl., Vol. 21, pp. 431-432.

Müller, O. Berichte der Bot. Gesell., p. 169, 1889; p. 70, 1897; p. 445, 1899.

Nägler, K. 1909. Entwicklungsgeschichtliche Studien über amöben. Arch. f. Protistenk., Vol. 15, pp. 1-53.

Nägeli, C. 1860. Ortsbewegungen der Pflanzenzellen und ihren Theilen. Beitr. z. wiss. Bot., Vol. 2, pp. 59-108.

Oppel, A. 1912. Über aktive Epithelbewegung. Anat. Anz., Vol. 41, pp. 400-409.

Ostwald, W. 1909. Grundriss der Kolloidchemie. Dresden.

Overton, E. 1907. Ueber den Mechanismus der Resorption und Sekretion. Handbuch Physiol., (Nagel) Vol. 2, pp. 744-898.

Pallas, P. S. 1766. Elenchus Zoophytorum.

Parks, G. J. 1903. On the thickness of the liquid film formed by condensation at the surface of a solid. Phil. Mag., Vol. 5, P. 517.

Pauli, W. 1908. Kolloidchemische Studien an Eiweiss. Kolloid-Zeit., Vol. 3, pp. 2-13.

Penard, E. 1902. Faune Rhizopodique du Bassin du Leman. Genève.

Penard, E. 1904. Quelques nouveaux Rhizopodes d'eau douce. Arch. f. Protistenk., Vol. 3, pp. 391-422.

v. Prowazek, S. 1909. Studien zur Biologie der Zellen. Biol. Centralbl., Vol. 19, pp. 291-296.

Przibram, H. 1913. Die Kammerprogression der Foraminiferen als Parallele zur Hautungsprogression der Mantiden. Arch. f. Entw.-Mech., Vol. 36, pp. 194-210.

Pütter, A. 1904. Die Flimmerbewegung. Ergebn. d. Physiol. Vol. 2, pp. 1-104.

Pütter, A. 1911. Vergleichende Physiologie. Jena.

Quincke, G. 1888. Über periodische Ausbreitung und dadurch hervorgerufene Bewegungserscheinungen. Annal. phys. Chem., Vol. 35, pp. 580-642.

Quincke, G. 1903. Die Oberflächenspannung an der Grenze wässeriger Kolloidlösungen von Verschiedener Koncentration. Annal. Physik, Vol. 10.

Reichert, E. T., and Brown, A. P. 1909. The differentiation and specificity of corresponding proteins and other vital substances in relation to biological classification and organic evolution. The crystallography of hemaglobins. Carnegie Institution Press. Washington.

Richet, C. 1902. De l'action anaphylactique de certains venins. C. R. Soc. Biol., Vol. 54, pp. 170-172.

Richet, C. 1912. L'Anaphylaxie. Paris, 286 pp.

Rhumbler, L. 1898. Physikalische Analyse von Lebenserscheinungen der Zelle. Arch. f. Entw.-Mech., Vol. 7, pp. 103-350.

Rhumbler, L. 1899. Physikalische Analyse und künstliche Nachahmung des Chemotropismus amöboider Zellen. Physik. Zeitschr., Vol. 1, pp. 43-47.

Rhumbler, L. 1899. Physikalische Analyse von Lebenserscheinungen der Zelle. Arch. f. Entw.-Mech., Vol. 9, pp. 32-62.

Rhumbler, L. 1899. Allgemeine Zellmechanik. Ergeb. der Anat., Vol. 8, pp. 543-625.

Rhumbler, L. 1902. Die Doppelschalen von Orbitolites und andere Foraminiferen, vom Entwicklungsmechanischen Standpunkt aus betrachtet. Arch. f. Protistenk., Bd. 1, pp. 193-296.

Rhumbler, L. 1905. Zur Theorie der Oberflächenkraft der Amöben. Zeit. f. wiss. Zoöl., Vol. 83, pp. 1-52.

Rhumbler, L. 1905. Der anomogene Oberflächenspannung des lebenden Zell-leibes. Anat. Hefte, Vol. 27, pp. 861-883.

Rhumbler, L. 1910. Die Verschiedenartigen Nahrungsaufnahmen bei Amö-ben als Folge Verschiedener Kolloidalzustände ihrer Oberflächen. Arch. f. Entw.-Mech., Vol. 30, pp. 194-223.

Rhumbler, L. 1914. Das Protoplasma als physikalisches System. Ergebn. d. Physiol., Vol. 14, pp. 474-617.

Robertson, T. B. 1905. An outline of the theory of the genesis of protoplasmic motion and excitation. Trans. Royal Soc. South Australia. Vol. 29, pp. 56.

Robertson, T. B. 1909. Remarks on the theory of protoplasmic movement and excitation. Quart. Journ. Exp. Physiol., Vol. 2, p. 303.

Rösel von Rosenhof, A. J. 1755. Insecten-Belustigung, 3 Vols. Nürnberg.

Sachs, J. v. 1865. Physiologie.

Schäfer, E. A. 1910. On McDougall's theory of muscular contraction. Quart. Journ. Exp. Physiol., Vol. 3, p. 63.

Schaeffer, A. A. 1910. Selection of food in Stentor caeruleus (Ehr). Jour. Exp. Zoöl., Vol. 8, pp. 75-132.

Schaeffer, A. A. 1914. Reactions of ameba to light. Science, Vol. 39, p. 474.

Schaeffer, A. A. 1916. On the feeding habits of ameba. Jour. Exp. Zoöl., Vol. 20, pp. 529-584.

Schaeffer, A. A. 1916. Concerning the species *Amoeba proteus*. Science, Vol. 44, pp. 468-469.

Schaeffer, A. A. 1916. On the behavior of ameba toward fragments of glass and carbon and other indigestible substances, and toward some very soluble substances. Biol. Bull., Vol. 31, pp. 303-337.

Schaeffer, A. A. 1917. On the reactions of ameba to isolated and compound proteins. Jour. Exp. Zoöl., Vol. 22, pp. 53-86.

Schaeffer, A. A. 1917. Choice of food in ameba. Jour. Anim. Behav., Vol. 7, pp. 220-258.

Schaeffer, A. A. 1917. Reactions of ameba to light and the effect of light on feeding. Journ. Exp. Zoöl., Vol. 32, pp. 45-74.

Schaeffer, A. A. 1917. On the third layer of protoplasm in ameba. Anat. Rec., Vol. 11, p. 477.

Schaeffer, A. A. 1918. Functional inertia in the movement of ameba. Anat. Rec., Vol. 14, p. 93.

Schaeffer, A. A. 1918. Three new species of amebas: *Amoeba bigemma* nov. spec., *Pelomyxa lentissima* nov. spec. and *P. Schiedti* nov. spec. Trans. Amer. Micros. Soc., Vol. 37, pp. 79-96.

Schardinger, F. 1899. Entwicklungskreis einer Amoeba lobosa, *Amoeba gruberi*.

S.-B. Akad. Berlin, Vol. 2, pp. 31-41.

Schaudinn, F. 1895. Über die Teilung von *Amoeba binucleata* Gruber. S.-B. Ges. Natur. Freunde, Berlin, pp. 130-141.

Schultz, E. 1915. Die Hyle des Lebens. Beobachtungen und Experimente an *Astrorhiza limicola*. Archiv. f. Entw.-Mech., Vol. 41, pp. 215-237.

Schulze, F. E. 1875. Rhizopodienstudien. IV. Archiv.. f. Mikros. Anat., Vol. 11. pp. 329-353.

Schepatieff, A. 1910. Amöbenstudien. Zoöl. Jahrb. Abt. Anat., Vol. 29, pp. 485-526.

Sharp, R. G. 1914. *Diplodinium ecaudatum* with an account of its neuromotor apparatus. Univ. Calif. Publ. Zoöl., Vol. 13, pp. 43-122.

Stahl, E. 1884. Zur Biologie der Myxomyceten. Bot. Ztg., Vol. 40, pp. 146-155, 162-175, 187-191.

Statkewitsch, P. 1903. Über die Wirkung der Induktionschläge auf einige Ciliata. Le Physiol. Russe, Vol. 3, pp. 41-45.

Strasburger, E. 1878. Wirkung des Lichtes und der Wärme auf Schwärmsporen. Jen. Zeit. Naturw., Vol. 551-625.

Štolc, A. 1900. Beobachtungen und Versuche über die Verdauung und Bildung der Kohlenhydrate bei einem amöbenartigen Organismus. Zeit. f. wiss. Zoöl., Vol. 68, pp. 625-668.

Štolc, A. 1910. Über kernlose Individuen und kernlose Teile von *Amoeba proteus*. Arch. f. Entw.-Mech., Vol. 29, pp. 152-168.

Thompson, D. W. 1917. On growth and form. Cambridge, England.

Torrey, H. B. 1907. The method of trial and the tropism hypothesis. Science, Vol. 26, pp. 313-323.

Torrey, H. B. and Hays, G. P. 1914. The role of random movements in the orientation of *Porcellio scaber* to light. Jour. Anim. Behav., Vol. 4, pp. 110-120.

v. Uexküll, J. 1909. Umwelt und Innenwelt der Tiere. Berlin.

Ulehla, V. 1911. Ultramikroscopische Studien über Geisselbewegung. Biol. Central., Vol. 31, pp. 645-654, 657-676, 689-705, 721-731.

Vahlkampf, E. Beiträge zur Biologie und Entwicklungsgeschichte von *Amoeba limax* einschliesslich der Züchtung auf Künstlichem Nährboden. Arch. f. Protistenk. Vol. 5, pp. 167-220.

Verworn, M. 1889. Psychophysiologische Protistenstudien. Jena.

Verworn, M. 1892. Die Bewegung der lebendigen Substanz. Jena.

Verworn, M. 1903. Die Biogenhypothese. Jena.

Verworn, M. 1909. Allgemeine Physiologie. Jena.

Wallich, G. C. 1863. On an undescribed undigenous form of Amoeba. Ann. and Mag. Nat. Hist., Vol. 11, p. 287.

Wallich, G. C. 1863. Further observations on an undescribed indigenous Amoeba. Ann. Mag. Nat. Hist., Vol. 11, pp. 365-371.

Wherry, W. B. 1913. Studies on the biology of an ameba of the limax group. Arch. f. Protistenk., Vol. 31, pp. 77-94.

Willis, H. S. 1916. The influence of the nucleus on the behavior of the ameba. Biol. Bull., Vol. 30, pp. 253-271.

Wilson, C. W. 1916. On the life history of a soil ameba. Univ. Calif. Publ. Zoöl., Vol. 16, pp. 241-292.

Wilson, H. V. 1900. Notes on a species of *Pelomyxa*. Amer. Nat., Vol. 34, pp.

Yocom, H. B. 1918. The neuromotor apparatus of *Euplotes patella*. Univ. Calif. Publ. Zoöl., Vol. 18, pp. 337-396.

Bayliss, W. M. 1915. Principles of General Physiology, London.

Craig, C. F. 1911. The parasitic amoebae of man. Philadelphia.

Gudger, E. W. 1916. On Leidy's *Ouramoeba* and its occurrence at Greensboro, N. C. Jour. Elisha Mitchell Scientific Soc., Vol. 32, pp. 24-32.

Hassell, A. 1912. Bibliography of parasitic amoebae. (Over 1000 titles). Trans. 15th Intern. Cong. Hygiene and Demography. Washington, 1913.

Jennings, H. S. 1916. Genetics, Vol. 1, pp. 407-543.

Jones, I. H. 1918. Equilibrium and Vertigo, 444 pp. 129 figs. Philadelphia.

Klemensievicz, R. 1898. Neue Untersuchungen über den Bau und die Thätigkeit des Eierzellen. Mitth. d. Vereins d. Ärzte in Steiermark. 35 Jahr., pp. 45-60.

Lynch, V. 1919. The function of the nucleus of the living cell. Amer. Jour. Physiol., Vol. 48, pp. 258-283.

Nuttall, G. F. 1901. Blood immunity and blood relationship. London.

Pfeffer, W. 1906. Physiology of plants. Trans. by A. J. Ewart, Oxford.

Schaeffer, A. A. 1917. Notes on the specific and other characters of *Amoeba proteus* (Leidy), *A. discoides* spec. nov., and *A. dubia* spec. nov. Arch. f. Protistenk. Vol. 37, pp. 204-228. 8 figs.

Schaeffer, A. A. 1919. Investigations on the specific characters of Marine Amebas at Tortugas. Year Book No. 18, Carnegie Inst. of Wash., pp. 204-205.

Todd, C. 1914. Recognition of the individual by hemolytic methods. Jour. Genetics, Vol. 3, pp. 123-130.

Velten, B. 1876. Aktiv oder passiv? Oester. Bot. Zeitschr.

Velten, B. 1876. Die physikalische Beschaffenheit des pflanzlichen Protoplasmas. S. B. d. Wiener Akad., Bd. 73.

Walton, L. B. 1918. Organic evolution and the significance of some new evidence bearing on the problem. Amer. Nat., Vol. 52, pp. 521-547.

Willows, R. S., and Hatscheck, E. 1916. Surface tension and surface energy. 2d ed. Philadelphia.

Lector House believes that a society develops through a two-fold approach of continuous learning and adaptation, which is derived from the study of classic literary works spread across the historic timeline of literature records. Therefore, we aim at reviving, repairing and redeveloping all those inaccessible or damaged but historically as well as culturally important literature across subjects so that the future generations may have an opportunity to study and learn from past works to embark upon a journey of creating a better future.

This book is a result of an effort made by Lector House towards making a contribution to the preservation and repair of original ancient works which might hold historical significance to the approach of continuous learning across subjects.

HAPPY READING & LEARNING!

LECTOR HOUSE LLP
E-MAIL: lectorpublishing@gmail.com

9 789389 560084